PHILOSOPHY
IN THE POETRY OF
Edwin Arlington Robinson

NUMBER 7 OF THE
COLUMBIA STUDIES IN
AMERICAN CULTURE

PHILOSOPHY
IN THE POETRY OF
Edwin Arlington Robinson

ESTELLE KAPLAN

AMS PRESS, INC.
NEW YORK
1966

AMS PRESS, INC.
New York, N.Y. 10003
1966

To F.M.K.

Acknowledgments

FOR PERMISSION to quote, the author is indebted to Mr. Lewis M. Isaacs, Mr. Louis V. Ledoux, and the Library of Harvard University, as well as to the Macmillan Company, the publishers of Robinson's poems and of Hermann Hagedorn's *Edwin Arlington Robinson*. For assistance and information in the pursuit of this study she is particularly grateful to Professor Daniel Gregory Mason, Professor Mark Van Doren, Mr. Ridgeley Torrence, and Mr. Hermann Hagedorn. The revision and editing of the manuscript is in large part the work of Mr. Boris Todrin, whose skill and knowledge have contributed much to the present form of this work. The author will always be indebted to Professor Herbert W. Schneider, who suggested the study. His patience, kindness, and helpfulness are those of a true philosopher and an inspiring teacher.

ESTELLE KAPLAN

New York
May 1, 1940

Contents

Part One : The Sources of
Robinson's Idealism

Biographical Clues

THE PUBLIC FACTS of Edwin Arlington Robinson's life are no adequate clues to the career of his mind, nevertheless they throw occasional light on the ideas embodied obscurely in his poetry. The appearance of Hermann Hagedorn's biography of Robinson has made it useless to repeat here the general course of his life—a life which throws less light on the problem of our inquiry than might be supposed. A few incidents described in his conversation and correspondence are worth noting here as clues to his guiding ideas. He was born in Head Tide, Maine, in 1869, he studied in the Gardiner (Maine) high school and spent two years at Harvard, which he entered in 1891. Much of his early life must be gleaned from a rather voluminous correspondence addressed in the main to close friends.[1] Letters sent to his school chum, Arthur R. Gledhill, are especially enlightening, revealing as they do something concerning his thought and studies between 1889 and 1896. In these years his handwriting still consisted of large, legible characters, which in later years were to fuse into the typical lines exemplified by the familiar *Tristram* manuscript.

In a letter of February 19, 1890, Robinson tells of going to dances and being pleased "to go to church when there is lots of singing." In mentioning the personal affairs of Gledhill he recommends that he marry, "for a minister needs someone

[1] The letters from which these quotations are taken are now in the Widener Library, Harvard University.

[3]

to keep his courage up during the dark days." His reply to an admonitory letter states,[2]

You know I am different from most people; is that why you wrote it? If she goes back on you, Art, all you will have to do is . . . become a skeptic, misanthrope, misogynist and pessimist and let the whole race of womankind go to the devil, or "dree your weird" through the lonely years consoling yourself with the poet's lines (not music)—

> " 'Tis better to have loved and lost
> Than never to have loved at all."

I wonder what the effect would be if I were to be caught in the same trap as yourself?—Basta! Basta! as Bulwer's Pocket Cannibal man [was] wont to say. . . 'Tis one of the best things ever written.

We find other characteristic expressions in this correspondence, such as, "if diabolical fiend Circumstance would permit it," interlarded with an abundance of latin quotations, many from Virgil's *Palaemon*, which he was translating at this time. Later in the year, having mentioned the little time spent in the society of girls, he continues:

Perhaps if I had something like your "anchor" to take up my thoughts, life would seem different, but [that] is hardly probable, and besides, Hypolito never meddled much with females. I guess there is no probable, possible shadow of doubt but that Gustavus Edward has glued his nose to the grindstone. Is he to be pitied or congratulated? But then there is no use in my beating around the bush at this rate; I will make my confession and leave you to judge me as you will. When we look back into the past and recall all the old scenes and incidents and friendships, some particular light must naturally shine brighter than others; some tender link that has joined the hearts of friends must take its strain in after days and the mighty question is at hand—will it yield?—or will it remain firm? I will deceive you no longer,—it yielded. I have left off

---

[2] February 23, 1889.

[4]

chewing tobacco! The last graduation and reception brought a train of thoughts into my head with the above result. Beats the devil, don't it?

He admits that his invalid father sometimes gave him the "blues." Of John Sanger, who was ill, he observes,

If one of our old set should drop out there would be something gone from our own lives. Longfellow says,

"Something is gone from nature since they died
And summer is not summer, nor can be."

Thus, at the age of twenty Robinson manifests both his characteristic sensitivity to problems of misfortune and his sense of the comedy of it all. There is an indication of the balance between his serious interests in literature and his ineffable "philosophical" humor, an adumbration of the tragic comedy in his later poems. One page may contain a topical witticism from the Collier magazine and a philosophical observation of Spinoza. When Gledhill complained that the last two years at school were wasted, Robinson disagreed; "You will realize that life was something before you came to Spencer . . . Better keep away from Spinoza or he will have you before you know it: Pantheism is too attractive for you to tamper with." And referring to high school days:

In after years, when we are fairly established in the arena (if we ever are) then memories of those days will come back, and we will regard them, not with contempt, but with a finer sense of realization of contentment than we have ever known yet. I may be wrong but what would life be worth if it was all absorbed in this feverish drudgery of business.

The patent sincerity of these earlier thoughts is substantiated by Robinson's later disregard for business and by his devotion to the making of poems which stress the value of man's inner activity, although to the practical world such an occupation may appear a wasteful failure. He mentions his literary pabulum; he is reading Shakespeare, Tennyson, and Edna Lyall's *Donovan*, which he considers a "fine thing."

It is interesting to note here that Robinson declined a principal's position in the high school because of his deficiency in mathematics. "I declined, and smoked a pipe. I did not curse myself for my ignorance but rather felt thankful that I know no less than I do. I am a philosopher withal and shall doubtless some day be rich in something or other." [3]

In the following, early triolet, under cover of a conventional, metrical scheme and in the ironic comment that accompanies it, he sounds notes other than the gay tones usual in *vers de société*.

By the way I made a triolet, yesterday; here it is:

> Silent they stand against the wall,
>   The mouldering boots of other days.
> No more they answer duty's call—
> Silent they stand against the wall,—
> Over their tops the cold bugs crawl,
>   Like distant herds o'er darkened ways,
> Silent they stand against the wall,
>   The mouldering boots of other days.

Observe the bucolic pathos and fine feeling. This form of verse is of French extraction. . . . They give a man a chance to pour out his whole soul (as I have done) in eight lines.[4] [And] I have these spells of moralizing occasionally and considering the sentiment expressed from the standpoint of psychological affinity, there may be some chance for an argument in its favor.[5]

After reading Hardy's *The Hand of Ethelberta, Far from the Madding Crowd*, and *Under the Greenwood Tree*, he writes,

[3] March 11, 1891.   [4] *Ibid.*   [5] April, 1891.

"There is a marvelous mixture of pastoral humor and pathos. Tragedy is by no means forgotten, though Hardy is not so bloodthirsty as his contemporary Blackmore." [6] At this time Hardy seemed to him peerless, and much of the pathos of Hardy and his romantically tinged conception of tragedy invaded Robinson's early work. One of his first published poems was a sonnet on Hardy.[7] Certainly the former's recognition of evil at least partially stems from the author of *Jude the Obscure* and *The Mayor of Casterbridge*. His reading, however, included Hawthorne's *Scarlet Letter*, Ruskin's *Humanity*, Eliot's *Middlemarch*, *Hamlet*, and, for diversion, Boccaccio and Petrarch. Symphonies and operas were also a source of joy to him.

On January 10, 1892, he admits, "I am in agony when I have nothing to kick against." In another letter,

Tomorrow (Saturday) evening, if the winds are right and the planets propitious, I will go into town and have a bottle of Guinness "Dublin" by way of Thanksgiving. I have been having these thanksgivings about every third night all through the mid-year season.[8]

This early habit of drinking was one he never discouraged, and it possessed him increasingly. *Dionysus in Doubt* is too vivid a portrayal of inebriate experience to find its source in anything but reality.

He complains of the French, Anglo-Saxon, and Shakespeare courses that were required at Harvard. Some students at the college "haven't picked up" anything. This was his feeling in October, 1891, but in September, 1892, he notes that he was studying the required Philosophy I, which included logic, psychology, and the history of philosophy; he also took courses in

---

[6] *Ibid.*   [7] See Hagedorn, *Edwin Arlington Robinson*, p. 98.
[8] March 11, 1891.

ancient art for his own "satisfaction." Simply because he mani-
fested a distaste for academic logic and psychology, it would
hardly be safe to infer that he "picked up" nothing from his
courses in Philosophy I. He had benefited considerably from
his study of the history of philosophy and from Royce's *The
Spirit of Modern Philosophy*, as we shall see. In a letter of March
21, 1893, speaking of logic, which he never enjoyed and to
which he refers as "worse than hell itself,"

You have given me to understand that you can learn logic; if
so, you are of a different clay from myself. It is well-nigh unintel-
ligible to me. It "soured" me on the whole course and now I find
Psychology about as bad. I do not think I was born for a philosopher even in as limited a sense as elementary psychology implies.
We are to study Royce's "Spirit of Modern Philosophy" for the
rest of the year. It ought to be interesting but I have not much courage. P.S. I wish you all success with your "cell." If it turns out to be
spelled with an "s" you can still be thankful that you have lived.
Remember what Aldrich says: "They fail, and they alone, who
have not striven." No charge.

This letter, of some importance to this inquiry for its reference
to Royce, resembles an earlier letter, September 20, 1892, which
mentions the following basic theme in his "moralizing":

I am beginning to feel a little guilty for not having done more for
myself in my life; but then there is no use in regretting what is past.
At least, that is what the prosperous ones tell us.

Although the prosperous caution failures against regret, not to
recall the spent years is well-nigh impossible. This letter indicates an obsession that grew on him. The "vanity" of regret was
preached by the prosperous person, because of his complacency; to the failure brooding over the past, regret is as inevitable as the dead hours are irrevocable. This observation, apparently casual, is one of his earliest comments on fatalism and

free will and reveals a tendency to accept fatalism ironically rather than literally. He had been reading *Tom Jones*, Blackmore's *Alice Lorraine*, and Balzac's *Eugénie Grandet*. "Some object to *MacLeod of Dare* on general principles, but the tragic end improves it for me."

On May 23, 1893, he refers to jobs: "Most of the people who have them seem to be better off than those who do not, but most of the people are not so hopelessly fettered by their individual tastes as I am." While he was taking courses in philosophy, he was also studying French, German, and English composition, and for the latter he was writing a theme on *Pendennis*. A letter of October 28, 1893 mentions his desire to write:

If I make a failure of it, and the chances are about ten to one that I shall, my life will be a disappointment and a failure. I do not know much about the ways of successful men and the thing called "business" was always a bugbear and a mystery to me. . . . If I had your general intellect and faculty of making yourself popular wherever you go, life would be a different thing for me. I have lived nearly twenty-four years, and am thankful chiefly that I haven't them to live over again. So you see my life hasn't been such a pleasant affair as some men's seem to be. Perhaps it is partly my own fault, but I hardly understand how it can be to any great extent.

That he feared failure less than he feared compromise is patent. His feeling for poetry and his essential confidence in his undertaking (realizing as he did the seriousness of his desire) made him indifferent to the opinion of others. This first definite expression of awareness of his worldly shortcomings, with its resulting disillusionment, reveals his tendency to avoid the flagellation of self-blame and to search for an external cause, such as destiny, although he has not yet used that name. Men who fail, disturb him, but he cannot solve the problem.

"Those were the good days," he says of his youth. Again recalling Cambridge, "I am a better man with better ideals than I was before I went, but I am afraid they are not the ideals to keep me in the active walk of life, whatever they may be." Robinson was always self-conscious concerning his material failure, as most people measure it. Although concerned with his own problems, he was considerate of those of others. Referring to his friend's new position, which he thought bad for him. he adds, "But it is the thing that was to be, so there is no use in conjecturing on what might have been the result, if he had done differently. More than that, I am hardly in a position to criticize anyone's actions."

As early as 1893 he is tinged with a type of resignation which later appeared in his poetry. In his letter of September 29, 1894, he says: "I am not ungodly nor irreligious, but there are a few things that I cannot stand." Nor is this inconsistent with his general attitude of acceptance. In December of the year he comments:

Sometimes I wonder if I am not a damned fool after all, and feel very queer as I meet my old friends all going by me in the race. Perhaps my time is coming—I rather think it is—but doubts are heavy and the devil seems to be the boss of things. However I work on in my own ridiculous way (like Bret Harte's "Dow") and manage to see now and then a glimpse of the show. I don't think it amounts to much, upon the whole, but I do not growl half so much as this letter may lead you to think. . . . Christmas has an effect upon me which I cannot describe—something like that of the first hand-organs in the spring—makes me feel hollow and vaguely conscious of wasted time, or as I prefer to call it, lost time.

His concerns with time, relative success, and doubt are, of course, dominant material for the poems. In the spring of the

following year Robinson is "feeling down at the heels. . . .
My courage is pretty good, however, and I do not mean to 'give
in' until I positively have to. . . . You will excuse my shortcomings on the ground of human nature." It is quite clear that
"blaming nature" is not escape for him.

On October 28, 1896, he refers to a poem that achieved the
"elevation" of print: "I sing, in my own particular manner, of
heaven and hell and now and then of material things (supposing they exist)." This is his first written expression, insofar as
we can determine of an idealistic conception of reality. In the
same vein:

I have been slowly getting rid of materialism for the past year or
two, but I fear I haven't the stamina to be a Christian—accepting
Christ as either human or divine. Selfishness hangs to a man like
a lobster—and is the thing that keeps humanity where it is. I
know that, but at present I am pretty much of a human being,
though I see a glimmer of the light once in a while and then medi-
tate on its possibilities.

This letter with its allusions to overcoming materialism and
seeing the light, is nearer his poetical themes than any other.
Characteristic, too, is his comment, "*The Night Before* is an attempt to be absolutely impersonal, which, of course, is an impossibility."

The point is not so much that Robinson is an idealist, as that
perhaps, through the influence of Royce, he is willing to allow
full range to the skepticism implicit in idealism rather than to
the dogmatic fatalism of materialism. His skepticism means that
one can never know, not that knowing is useless. The puritan
trait seems to indicate that in his letters, as in his poems, he is
talking not only about material things but also about heaven
and hell in the human soul. He is carrying on the gospel of

Emerson and of New England deepened by an idealistic appreciation of pessimism. His conscience is "New England" and is preoccupied with his own spiritual state—his soul; it is in truth a spiritual selfishness "that hangs to a man like a lobster," especially in New England. This combination of puritanism, transcendentalism, and pessimism (Hawthorne, Emerson, and Hardy) gradually crystallized into a permanent pattern for his poetry, but it was at the same time an expression of his "New England conscience," as is evident in the following lines:

> Let us, the Children of the Night,
> Put off the cloak that hides the scar!—
> Let us be Children of the Light,
> And tell the ages what we are! [9]

Letters [10] to Daniel Gregory Mason reveal again Robinson's reading and his critical acumen, penetrating to the heart of the matter in hand. On June 19, 1889, he writes from Cambridge:

I stretched out yesterday and read *Walking* [Thoreau's essay], but did not quite relish what seemed to me to be a sort of glorified world-cowardice all through the thing. For God's sake says the sage, let me get away into the wilderness where I shall not have a single human responsibility or the first symptom of social discipline. Let me be a pickerel or a skunk cabbage, or anything that will not have to meet the realities of civilization. There is a wholesomeness about some people that is positively unhealthy, and I find it in this essay. Still I am ready for *Walden*.

Robinson was now also reading Emerson's *The Conduct of Life*, which he thought should be read before the *Essays*.

In the essay on Power he takes me over his paternal knee and wallops me with a big New England shingle for about three quar-

---

[9] Quoted in Hagedorn, *Edwin Arlington Robinson*, p. 101.
[10] *The Yale Review*, XXV (June, 1936), 860–64.

ters of a New England hour. He really gets after me: "A day is a more magnificent cloth than any muslin, the mechanism that makes it is infinitely cunninger, and you shall not conceal the sleezy, fraudulent, rotten hours you have slipped into the piece; nor fear that any honest thread, or straighter steel, or more inflexible shaft, will not testify in the web." [Referring to his changed ideas of Emerson's humanity and humor] I am ready to confess, however, that the human note has a faint suggestion of falsetto here and there, but, on the other hand may not that suggestion be the product of my own diabolical system rather than of Emerson's idealism?

In 1897, following his Cambridge days, Robinson had a good opportunity for expanding and expounding his own "diabolical system" when he was joined in a New York rooming house by his college friend George Burnham. Of this episode Hermann Hagedorn writes:

Burnham had achieved an Oriental tolerance illuminated by an Occidental sense of humor, and helped Robinson cut the last of the hawsers that bound his spirit to "the crumbled wharves" of accepted theology. "The tap-root of the subconscious goes down to God," he would say. "There is only one self. That we call God, or the Absolute. Everything is the manifestation of that Absolute." Robinson followed his thought without accepting his phrasing. Night after night, at some cafe off Columbus Circle, they discussed the Absolute, over beers.[11]

From Irving Place, on October 30, 1899, Robinson notes: "I have just finished *Wuthering Heights* by Emily Brontë and feel as if I had digested a thunder-storm. It is a book of genius, but not the kind of genius that makes men grow. . . . Clearness and elegance are left out but there is force enough to run a saw-mill." Politics, Roosevelt, and McKinley are mentioned when he writes that, "Up to a fortnight ago I did not intend to

11 Hagedorn, *Edwin Arlington Robinson*, p. 131.

vote for anybody but I changed my mind—to the great delight of one Miss Rich, who thinks she did it. If any more political females come to this house I shall have to move back to Harlem." Returning from the limbo of politics, he asks Mason to write an overture to *The Birds* of Aristophanes. He was expecting Moody to dine with him— "One can do very well at Riggs's for a quarter—provided he has faith. To him that hath shall be given, but it depends a good deal on how much he hath." From records in the Customs House, Port of New York in 1909, we learn that holding a job makes him feel like a prisoner, especially,

. . . as I am in a mood for work (work with me means studying the ceiling and my navel for four hours and then writing down perhaps four lines—sometimes as many as seven and again none at all) while there is just enough going on here, not to mention all hell outside, to keep my poor relic of a brain in a state that suggests nothing to me at this moment unless it be a state of semi-agitated punk. Yes, punk's the word with me; and it will be for some time to come unless I can contrive to hypnotize my chief officer into an appreciation of my place in nature. If I come in some afternoon and find him waving a 'phony' invoice in one hand and Old Doctor Moody's "Masque of Judgment" in the other, I shall know that I have the right kind of an eye for him. . . . On the other hand don't you make the mistake of supposing that I have failed, or do fail, to appreciate my devilish good luck in landing here. My chief concern is a fear that I may turn out a disappointment to my friends and to T. R.—who must be wondering, if he finds time, how long it takes a man to write a hundred pages of verse. It does not, in fact, take long to write a hundred pages of verse, but, unfortunately, there is only a visual resemblance between verse and the other thing. For quantity (I mean size) I do not myself care a damn; but a fellow has to be dead before the public understands that a dozen titles are quite enough to string wires on that will reach through ten times as many centuries—

perhaps. I don't know about my metaphor, nor do I know that I have ever done anything that the future will require, but I do know that those things I have done are my own (to use the world's nonsense) and that they have to be done in my way. If they go by the board, they will go because I could not build them any better. Now that this exquisite bit of drivel is out of my system, I'll have a smoke.

Letters to Amy Lowell, written at the end of Robinson's career, when he had attained recognition, even though it was not as thoroughly approving as he might have desired, reveal him as still apologetic about his material failure as compared with the success of men in business and other professions. In the letter of October 22, 1914, he explains that writing poetry justifies his existence and that he is therefore at work. In the following year he writes,

I formed the habit when I was a small child when I used to rock myself in a chair many sizes too large for me and wonder why the deuce I should have ever been born. I was indignant about it for years, but I've got well over that—though I may not have answered my own question in all ways to my own satisfaction.

On March 18, 1916, referring to Miss Lowell's criticism of his latest poem, *The Man against the Sky:*

Nothing could have been further from my mind when I wrote "The Man" than any emissary of gloom or of despair. In the closing pages, I meant merely, through what I supposed to be an obviously ironic medium, to carry materialism to its logical end and to indicate its futility as an explanation or a justification of existence.

He continues in another letter, referring to criticism in the *New Republic:*

I agree with most of them, although I don't believe that I'm a pessimist. It is one thing to see the world at all or rather to see it as it

[15]

isn't (after the manner of many optimists), and another to see it [as] it is, or as it seems to be. But this is merely a quibble.

Later he says, "In looking over my life I find that I have no life to speak of, much less to write about." This statement is but one link in the armor of his reticence. There are, to be sure, other remarks imbued with the inscrutable humor: "I am some sort of a New England shellfish—probably a Maine clam."

During what may be called the second period of his thinking, the period when he had arrived, but was defending his position with epistolary shrapnel to friends, Robinson wrote an introduction to several books and letters and an article called "The Peterborough Idea." [12] After his experiences at Harvard, in Harlem, and in the New York Customs House, he lived in a new environment, which made an important change in his habits. For several years he was invited to the MacDowell Colony, at Peterborough, New Hampshire. From 1911 until his death he spent his summers at the "Colony," a word which had been obnoxious to him before he went there. The MacDowell Colony, he said, gave him the opportunity to get away from the world and

express a part of what the world had given me. . . . [The place] compels a man to work out the best that is in him, and to be discontented if he fails to do so. . . . For the world must have its art, or the world will be no fit place to live in; and the artist must have his opportunity, or his art will die.

In this article he speaks of his New England conscience as a long-suffering one that had never bothered him about lost opportunity. Further evidence of Robinson's views concerning failure in its relation to peace is contained in his note on Thoreau's correspondent Myron B. Benton.

[12] *The North American Review*, CCIV (September, 1916), 448–54.

99 St. Botolph Street
Boston, April 20, 1921—

Dear Griffith:—

I am sorry to leave New York without seeing you and Mrs Griffith again, but was called away rather suddenly and so just didn't get around to it. When I had been here about a week it occurred to me that your Lawrence book was still at 28 West 8th Street, and I began to wonder what you must think of me. Unfortunately I shall not be in New York again until next November, when I expect to be with the Frasers again in their new place in 42nd Street.

Thank you for liking that sonnet and for reprinting some of them. I hope you may succeed in doing the first poem in the book — It should stand rather a chance in your venture.

Yours sincerely,

E. A. Robinson

LETTER TO WILLIAM GRIFFITH

Like many an unassuming man before him, the late Myron B. Benton may be said to have been predestined by a sort of casual immortality. If we could know the whole truth of the matter, perhaps we should know to our surprise and possible discomfiture that all so-called earthly remembrance, is casual or accidental, or what you will. At any rate, we all know that many who have failed in their special attempt have worked harder and longer than many who have attained to that uncertain and often unsatisfying thing called success; and perhaps it is better for our vanity and our peace of mind that most of us do not waste much of our time in wondering whether a man is born to be what he is, or whether it is he that makes himself what he is. It may be the kind of illusion of a special providence that permits most of us, at least to a considerable extent, to assume the latter inference to be true, or it may be nothing of the sort.[13]

Robinson approved of Thoreau's "one world at a time," but he appreciated Benton's "O God, is there another world so sweet" not at all. Benton was a "rare soul" and a true son of the earth in the very best sense. He says of Benton, "with all his talents, which were by no means inconsiderable, his fate might still be that of a happily-earned obscurity, but for his poignant and unique letter from Thoreau and for his long and intimate correspondence with John Burroughs."

While his letters to Miss Lowell bear a tone of apologetic antagonism or at least disagreement, those to Arthur Davison Ficke show him to be very modest in asking people to read his work and grateful for their services. It is interesting to note that by this time his handwriting has progressed from open legibility to cramped illegibility.

A letter of July 9, 1917, from the MacDowell Colony where

[13] *Thoreau's Last Letter,* with a note on his correspondent, Myron B. Benton, pp. 9–12.

he was passing the summer, states:

I am sending you a copy of "Merlin," which seems to have a refrigerating effect on most of the critics. Miss Monroe, for example, cannot even tell when I am trying to be entertaining. Purgatory is, I fancy, the place where all one's jokes are taken seriously. This makes me think of F. P. A.'s "What's the use of being subtle, as Cain said to Abel."

Another letter from Peterborough mentions that his *Lancelot* was not as "difficult" to follow as *Merlin*. "I supposed that M. was clear as daylight (which isn't always very clear), and I'm glad at any rate that you succeeded in liking the Vivian part."

Critics' Comments

INTERPRETATIONS other than those gleaned from his own letters may be mentioned briefly, though they are for the most part not very well informed and not detailed enough to throw much light on our present inquiry. At least they suggest the need for a critical examination of Robinson's philosophical ideas. B. R. Redman, criticizing *The Torrent and the Night Before* in the *Bookman*,[1] 1897, said, "His humor is of a grim sort, and the world is not beautiful to him, but a prison-house." Robinson replied, "The world is not a 'prison-house,' but a kind of spiritual kindergarten where bewildered infants are trying to spell God with the wrong blocks." Later, during an interview with Nancy Evans, when the phrase was recalled to him, "He said, with a sort of fond disapproval, 'I was young then and it was a smart thing to say.'" But the thought was not lost on Mr. Redman, who saw that it "compacted the tragedy, the humor, the pity, and the doubt that are vitalizing elements of Robinson's utterance."

In December 21, 1919, the book review section of the New York *Times*, laureled him with a collective article, "Poets Celebrate Edwin Arlington Robinson's Fiftieth Birthday." Louis Ledoux praised him with:

Intense sympathy with those who have suffered misfortune—mental, physical or moral; the desire to feel with all men under all circumstances, but especially in the crises of failure and unhappi-

---

[1] See Evans, "Record of an Interview," *The Bookman*, LXXV (November, 1932), 680.

ness; insistence upon the possible nobility of those who seem ignoble, unbeautiful—these are to me the bases of Robinson's poetry.

He sees the happiness that might be, never the happiness that is; but as the poet of the unattained he is unrivaled in clearness of perception and exquisite tenderness of understanding.

George Sterling gave his pacific greeting: "The only poet whose truth is always beauty and whose beauty is always truth." Josephine Preston Peabody: "A master etcher of human portraits." Hermann Hagedorn: "Life—humorous, grave, sordid, wistful, terrible in detail, but never altogether without hope—rises and falls with the inevitability of the tides through his lines."

Much of the later criticism varies. F. J. Mather [2] said that Robinson maintains "along with this tragic sense of life a wistful and expectant hopefulness." William Rose Benét,[3] who knew Robinson in New Hampshire, found him "laconic and Olympian," as kind, generous and lovable as his poem on Lincoln. The appreciation of Robinson in the *New Republic* is amusingly inconsistent. It states that the problem of "what does it mean" is answered in his poems and remarks that

The trouble was that his two high virtues—call them dignity and honesty—ended by interfering with each other. The honesty caused him to write poems that were sometimes undignifiedly prosaic. The dignity forced him to lead a restricted and impoverished life, and thereby cut him off from the world of his time; without taking part in it, he could not answer the question, "What does it mean?" [4]

In an editorial in the *Nation* it seemed to trouble the anonymous editor very much, that Edwin Arlington Robinson

---

[2] *The Saturday Review of Literature*, VI (January 11, 1930), 629.
[3] *Ibid.*, XI (April 13, 1935), 628.
[4] [Editorial], "The Week," *The New Republic*, LXXXII (April 17, 1935), 268–69.

did nothing while he lived to ingratiate any conceivable public. Not merely did he refuse to toss us the customary information about his personal life, but the very poetry he gave us to read in twenty volumes was agnostic in temper and austere in tone.[5]

The editorial continued with a discussion of the narratives, from *Merlin* in 1917 to *Amaranth* in 1934; this at least is more germane to the matter in hand.

Is the music in them too coldly overlaid with intelligence? Are they also enduring? If they are, then Robinson is a major poet. . . . If they are not, the reason will probably have been that their famous blank-verse line had too much steel in it and too little gold; that it was sharper than it was lovely . . . more particularly toward the end, too little of a poetic line and too narrowly a vehicle for the transmission of thought.

The poet has generally been interpreted in terms of his physical haunts. "Tilbury Town" *must* have been Gardiner, Maine, where he spent his boyhood; "The Town Down the River"—why, of course, that *was* New York. Keeping him a New England poet was the first step; making him a New England philosopher followed naturally enough. Apropos of this hypothesis, Percy Mackaye said no other poet has "revealed a soul more nakedly New England even when most universal in its vesture." [6] Amy Lowell observed his "Puritan weakness in fighting sorrow" and his "protest against brutal, unfeeling materialism." Charles Cestre called Robinson a descendant of the Puritans, a moralist, a mystic like Emerson. The idea of singing while in pain, as we find it in *Captain Craig*, is contrary to rea-

[5] [Editorial], "Edwin Arlington Robinson," *The Nation*, CXL (April 17, 1935), 434.
[6] Book review section of *The New York Times*, December 21, 1919, p. 2.

soned thought but in accordance with Puritan tradition and wholly possible in a poem. "Amour et sympathie sont à la base de cette philosophie de la joie, qui s'alimente aux sources de l'harmonie universelle." [7]

Edwin Markham ventured a similar exposition:

Perhaps his most striking note is his awareness of the mystery of life—the Fates using men as foils. He has no preachment for us; or if he has, it appears to urge us to meet Fate head-on, with high-heart, knowing that this lofty attitude will suffice whether we only go down to dust, or ascend at last to higher destinies. [8]

Similarly Untermeyer in *Modern American Poetry* analyzed Robinson's poetry as "a manifest searching for the truth, for the light beyond illusion."

The continental critics include Karl Arns, who sees Robinson progressively stripping off his faith in life and reality but clinging to a faith in truth. "Dieser Glaube ist nur ein Schimmer in aller Dunkelheit, aber dieser Schimmer genüght. . . . Er

[7] L'Œuvre poétique d'Edwin Arlington Robinson, *Revue Anglo-Américaine*, Paris, 1924, p. 281. A course in the poetry of Edwin Arlington Robinson has been given by Cestre at Harvard.
Cestre continues:
"Le poète, qui contemple ce personnage, symbole de l'humanité, en route vers les confins fulgurants de l'univers, vibre de l'émoi qui agite l'âme puritaine à la pensée du voyage vers la frontière invisible où la vie rencontre le destin. . . . C'est dans la tradition de la polémique idéaliste des Puritains, témoins Carlyle et Bernard Shaw. . . . Il ne subit plus l'autorité du dogme; mais son âme religieuse s'élève spontanément à la foi en l'Etre Suprême et en l'immortalité. . . . Il est soutenu, au milieu des doutes qui l'assaillent ou des pensées sombres qui lui suggère le spectacle du monde, par la voix miraculeuse descendue des hauteurs où l'âme communie avec l'infini. . . . Cette voix lui apporte l'assurance que, si notre époque (plus éclairée déjà que les âges barbares) cherche encore à tâtons la vérité, le progrès moral se dévoilera un jour dans une révélation éclatante, accompagnée des accents augustes de la genèse d'un monde. . . . Cette foi donne au penseur la force de faire face aux questions angoissantes que la lucidité de son intelligence suscite à chaque détour du chemin de la vie."
[8] Book review section of *The New York Times*, December 21, 1919, p. 2.

kennt keinen leidsuchenden und keinen leidüberwindenden Idealismus." [9]

Ridgely Torrence, poet and lifelong friend of Robinson, stated to the author that Robinson was not interested in the metaphysics of the schools, but that he had a keen survey of the fruits of philosophy—that at Harvard he did not know Santayana and had no course with him. It is impossible, Mr. Torrence maintained, to trace his derivations, although the nearest he came to sitting at someone's feet was in his early 'teens when he was writing verse under the tutelage of the family physician. Robinson would say, that what he got from Harvard was a kind of cultural background from the air he breathed —not from the classroom. Though Robinson greatly appreciated Schopenhauer, being both amused and impressed by him, he saw, according to Mr. Torrence, horizons far beyond Schopenhauer's.

[9] *Germanisch-Romanische Monatsschrift*, XII (1924), 224–29. The review continues:

"Whitman soll die Wirklichkeit verwandt haben, um den Bau seines idealistischen Glaubens zu errichten, während Robinson die Illusion Schicht nach Schicht von der Wirklichkeit abstreife, um uns bezüglich seiner Auffassung von Mensch und Schicksal ganz im unklaren zu lassen.

Vor einer innerlich unwahren Romantik bewahrt ihn sein grimmiger Wahrheitsdrang, vor einem öden Fatalismus und Pessimismus der Glaube, dass das Leben doch irgendeinen, obschon unerkennbaren Sinn haben müsse. . . . Und aus allen seinen Versen empfängt man den Eindruck unbedingter Ehrlichkeit und Aufrichtigkeit. . . .

Er scheint also an eine jenseits der menschlichen Erkenntnissphäre liegende Welt zu glauben. [e. g.] *The Man against the Sky.*

Ein Zwiespalt klafft in Robinson's Weltanschauung, das zeigt auch die ganz verschiedene Art, wie er seine beiden Arthur-Legenden ausklingen lässt—in Merlin 'there was a darkness over Camelot'—in Lancelot hoffnungsfroher—'and in the darkness came the Light.'

Er kennt keinen leidsuchenden und keinen leidüberwindenden Idealismus, Er beobachtet das Leben mit peinlicher Sorgfalt, deutet seine Äusserungen bis in alle Einzelheiten und findet es von intensivem psychologischen Interrese. Wie er Sympathie Empfindet, ist diese zumeist nur vage angedeutet. . . . Ein schöpfersicher Dichterphilosoph."

Royce and Schopenhauer

ALL SEEM TO AGREE that the New England transcendentalists exerted a strong influence on Robinson, though few concur on the nature of that influence. The controversy over the influence of Royce on his idealism leaves the question rather obscure and in addition makes his relation to Puritan tradition all the more debatable.

Lloyd Morris has made the most ambitious attempt to reveal the poet's connection with Puritan tradition and with transcendental idealism and, finally, with the idealism of Royce. According to Morris, Robinson's method was "to illuminate the present moment by revealing it as an inescapable reaping of the totality of a past. . . ." [1] Thus *Merlin* discloses "humanity in its eternal and universal aspects expressing those moods and aspirations which men, everywhere, have profoundly shared." [2] It concerns itself further with "race ideas and race memory" and "tends to conventionalize the pattern of life in a traditional symbolism." He was influenced by Emerson and, in particular, by the transcendentalist theory "that all human beings are part of one infinite life, and that the ends of this Absolute are best served through the cultivation by each individual of his special aptitudes." [3] This position adopted by Robinson suggests "the validity of individual insight and thereby counsels a certain tolerance in our moral judgments." [4] Turning from his quest

---

[1] Morris, *The Poetry of Edwin Arlington Robinson*, p. 13.
[2] *Ibid.*, p. 14.   [3] *Ibid.*, p. 38.   [4] *Ibid.*, pp. 38-39.

of influences for the moment, Mr. Morris comes closer to an interpretation of Robinson's poems, when he sees Robinson preoccupied in a "quest for certainty," which is "an adventure determined in part by our inheritance of the Puritan tradition and in part also by the critical temper of the modern mind." [5] Mr. Morris enlarges on his primary concept:

The Puritan theology stamped indelibly upon the New England mind the conviction that somehow every life represented a fresh chance for ultimate salvation; coupled with this individualism was a predisposition to speculation concerning the validity of our perceptions of experience and its ultimate significance. With the decline in intellectual influence of the Puritan creed, the speculative tendency of its genius cast itself adrift first and tentatively upon empirical philosophy, which it found deficient, if not sterile, in spiritual nourishment, and then upon the sea of German idealism, which, although it revived the native individualism of the Puritan genius, did not humiliate its relations with Divinity.[6]

The idealist philosophy of the transcendentalists required Josiah Royce to furnish a "rationalized interpretation of life."

And now Mr. Morris deals directly with Royce's philosophy and its specific influences.

Royce felt the burdens of a complicated world in which both error and evil seemed to be predominant. It was, perhaps, the modern mind's criticism of pure faith which impelled him to prove the existence of the Absolute through the existence of error. And it was characteristic of his moralistic tendency to find in evil an expression of the will of a perfect and omnipotent Absolute; a kind of shadow against which the contrasting high light of virtue rejoiced the aesthetic sense of the Absolute.

It is easy to see why Royce's romantic idealism, compounded of the transcendental individualism inherited from the Puritan tradition and the old Calvinistic intuition of original sin, should

---

[5] Morris, *The Poetry of Edwin Arlington Robinson*, p. 64.   [6] *Ibid.*

have offered a consolation and a refuge to many troubled spirits beyond that of a traditional religion by which they were not very profoundly moved. And it is undoubtedly true that Royce's sincerity, his earnest faith, and his fierce enthusiasm for final certitude left an abiding impression upon several generations of men who were students at Harvard when he held a chair of philosophy in that university. Mr. Robinson, who was at Harvard during that period, reveals in his poems a very definite preoccupation with the implications of the metaphysics of idealism.[7]

In discussing Morris's argument concerning the influence of Royce, Miss Nancy Evans, has this to say:

This is reasonable enough, to be sure, but unfortunately for so tidy an explanation the young Robinson did not know Josiah Royce. He told me that he thinks he was uninfluenced by any of the faculty; far from being absorbed in the metaphysics of idealism, he was revelling in the company of those young men who were his friends. "No," he said, "I'm afraid Mr. Morris was on the wrong track." Having said that, he smiled and added, "But if you want to find out about my 'Transcendentalism' [the quotes were in his voice] read *The Man against the Sky* and *Matthias at the Door*—it's in those poems." So did he recognize the aptness of Mr. Morris's conclusion while disagreeing with the argument . . . "It is impossible to believe that it is all for nothing—such waste would be inconceivable." [8]

That this indirect reply to Lloyd Morris is inadequate, must be evident from the early letters of Edwin Arlington Robinson which we have quoted above, as well as from internal evidence of his thought. It is to a more careful examination of this problem that we now turn.

It will be recalled that Robinson wrote early of studying Royce's *The Spirit of Modern Philosophy*. The course and the

[7] *Ibid.*, p. 66.
[8] Evans, "Record of an Interview," *The Bookman*, LXXV (November, 1932), 679.

book which resulted from it were dominated by the problem of pessimism as formulated by Schopenhauer. Royce's sympathetic treatment of this problem is worth noting here. The quoted passage is almost Robinson's thought in prose:

The world is, on the whole, very nearly as tragic as Schopenhauer represents it to be. Only spirituality consists in being heroic enough to accept the tragedy of existence, and to glory in the strength wherewith it is given to the true lords of life to conquer this tragedy, and to make their world after all divine. The way to meet Schopenhauer's pessimism is, not to refute its assertions, but to grapple practically with its truths. And if you do so, you will find as the real heart and significance of Schopenhauer's own gloomy thought, a vital, yes, even a religious assurance, which will make you thank God, that, as we tried to suggest by a phrase quoted in an earlier lecture, the very ice and cold, the very frost and snow, of philosophy praise and magnify him forever.[9] . . . On the contrary, I think that the best man is the one who can see the truth of pessimism, can absorb and transcend that truth, and can be nevertheless an optimist, not by virtue of his failure to recognize the evil of life, but by virtue of his readiness to take part in the struggle against this evil.[10] . . . Striving might be bearable were there a highest good, to which, by willing, I could attain, and if, when I once attained that good, I could rest. But if will makes the world and is the whole life and essence of it, then there is nothing in the world deeper than the longing, the unrest, which is the very heart of all willing. Doesn't this unrest seem tragic? Is there to be no end of longing in the world? If not, how can mere striving, mere willing, come to seem bearable? Here is the question which leads Schopenhauer to his pessimism.[11] . . . But is this the whole story? No; if we ever get our spiritual freedom, we shall, I think, not neglecting this caprice which Schopenhauer found at the heart of things, still see that the world is divine and spiritual, not so much in spite of this capriciousness, as just because of it. Caprice isn't all of reason; but

---

[9] Royce, *The Spirit of Modern Philosophy*, p. 230.
[10] *Ibid.*, p. 231.   [11] *Ibid.*, p. 260.

[28]

reason needs facts and passions to conquer and to rationalize, in order to become triumphantly rational. The spirit exists by accepting and by triumphing over the tragedy of the world. Restlessness, longing, grief,—these are evils, fatal evils, and they are everywhere in the world; but the spirit must be strong enough to endure them. In this strength is the solution. And, after all, it is just endurance that is the essence of spirituality. Resignation, then, is indeed part of the truth,—resignation, that is, of any hope of a final and private happiness. We resign in order to be ready to endure. But courage is the rest of truth,—a hearty defiance of the whole hateful pang and agony of the will, a binding of the strong man by being stronger than he, a making of life once for all our divine game, where the passions are the mere chessmen that we move in carrying out our plan, and where the plan is a spiritual victory over Satan. Let us thank Schopenhauer, then, for at least this, that in his pessimism he gives us an universal expression for the whole negative side of life.[12]

There may not be very much similarity between Schopenhauer and Robinson, but there certainly is between Robinson and the Roycean interpretation of Schopenhauer, particularly in the point of view that solution of evil lies in endurance, not in defining it. The mirror of life, reflecting its "whole negative side," caught at the same time the innate courage and guidance of an enduring light; and, looking at the dark glass, Robinson saw the shadow and the beam.

In any interpretation of Royce and of Robinson it is of primary importance to observe the distinction between transcending good and evil and facing good and evil. Of the latter interpretation of the Roycean Absolute, Morris is not fully aware. Instead of overcoming finite evil in the manner of the earlier transcendental optimism, Royce admits that evil, too, is infinite, and hence the struggle against it is also infinite—an integral aspect of God's life. Instead of denying the eternal reality

[12] *Ibid.*, pp. 263–64.

of evil, one must struggle eternally with God against it. For Royce, evils do exist, but the "spirit must be strong enough to endure them." This spirit of courage is the Absolute.

In general critics have succeeded in pointing to the problem, but the Roycean interpretation of Schopenhauer, as an element in the philosophy of Robinson, has been merely found, not defined. Babette Deutsch approaches the idea in a groping review of *Cavender's House*. She refers to Robinson's "resigned if sorrowful agnosticism." Mark Van Doren finds him consistent in "his presentation of the problem which existence is." And with Robinson's own imagery, rather than logical precision, this same critic sees in the poem "a little light in a great deal of darkness, a wisp of music in a universe of irregular drums." These images, he tells us, Mr. Robinson uses for "portraying man's never quite wholly vain struggle for self-respect." [13]

Percy Hutchinson regards Robinson's sympathy with "fate moving from the centre to the periphery of a man's life," as the key concept in the poet's thought. "Perhaps it is a result of a double distillation of crude Darwinism synthesized with Calvinism plus a dash of the wisdom of Greece. Yet although it is the foundation-stone on which Robinson erects the pinnacle of his thought, he is not averse to poking a bit of questing fun at the entire edifice . . . lines to Ampersand, a decidedly supernatural cat." [14]

Robinson himself tells us that unlike Thoreau (and Schopenhauer, for that matter) he was willing to meet the realities of morality in society and civilization. However, he followed Emerson's (Thoreau's and Schopenhauer's) individualism, rather than Royce's absolutism, though without Emerson's op-

[13] Miss Evans refers to these critics of Robinson in "Record of an Interview," *The Bookman*, LXXV (November, 1932), 675–81.
[14] Book review section of *The New York Times*, April 21, 1935, p. 11.

timistic self-confidence; as for self-reliance, that was always his. Robinson thinks of "courage" in the most solitary terms and of knowledge as self-knowledge in a strictly individualistic sense. His "own diabolical system," was a reinterpretation of Emerson, sobered by taking nature seriously and tragically. The preoccupation with self-knowledge becomes—in his own system—a meditation on one's fate. He keeps the individual's idealism in a materialistic setting so that the meaning of existence must be the absoluteness of one's defiance. Retaining the egocentric predicament in a materialistic setting, he attained a form of stoicism which was distinctly more philosophic than the current literary "realism." The seeker of the light is precisely the idealist seeking himself in a world of material forces.

Robinson must have been influenced to some extent by Hardy's critiques, as well as by those of Royce and Schopenhauer, in repudiating Emerson's optimistic idealism. Royce believed that good and evil, which are infinite and contradictory, cannot be reconciled; therefore it follows that we can understand only formally the meaning of the phrase "God eternally reconciles them." Emerson took the meaning in life to be whatever meaning any individual finds in it; Royce took it to be whatever God finds.

Certainly Robinson's general background and thought (the stuff of which he may have pulled out of the cultural atmosphere, rather than from textbooks) were in terms of New England transcendentalism, especially as formulated by Emerson. Against this he projected his concepts of materialism—more nearly Spencer's theory of evolution than Darwin's. The implications of materialism troubled him greatly, for this materialism negated Emerson's thought. Then Schopenhauer, filtering through Royce and distilled further in the alembic of

Hardy's world, struggling against indifferent, albeit neutral forces, presents another type of idealism—an idealism derived from an examination of evil and error. This resulted in the Roycean loyalty to the light, though it reveals nothing to the finite mind. When Emerson asked, "what does the world mean," he derived all sorts of meaning; when Robinson did this, he knew all kinds of doubt. Robinson thought he had quite finished with Emerson, but after he read Royce he returned to the former, especially to *The Conduct of Life*, with renewed understanding.

Two Sonnets [15] express succinctly this transition from both conventional idealism and conventional materialism to his absolutistic agnosticism. The first sonnet refers to materialism and idealism as "the two-fold screen of twisted innocence" and the second sonnet ends on the theme that moral knowledge must wait

> Till we have drunk, and trembled at the taste,
> The mead of Thought's prophetic endlessness.

Self-Knowledge

Like his friend Moody—and Santayana, Robinson was a member of a group of sad men. In *The Last Puritan* there is such a group. It is difficult to ascertain the degree of influence Santayana had over Robinson; it is possible that he had no influence whatsoever, negative or positive, inasmuch as the evidence is obscure. However, Santayana's sonnets reflect the same thought one finds in Robinson and reveal the general intellectual and moral "atmosphere" of Harvard Yard in the early nineties.

Robinson places emphasis on the futility of materialism as a

[15] Robinson, *Collected Poems*, 1934, p. 89.

"justification of existence." When in his rare interviews, and more intimately in his correspondence he does mention his philosophy, he denies adherence to any brand of pessimism. Similarly, he is in no sense a materialist; he is always in search of self-understanding. He clings to the ideal of self-understanding, although it acquires various hues as he becomes older. In his first period, he emphasized "realism" in the Hardian sense—an attempt to see life as "it really is." And, cryptic though his reflection may be, it is there to yield its ore to the persistent digger. In this early period of his thought Robinson was sharply influenced by Schopenhauer's concept of the transcendence of will by idea; the evil world of will is transcended only by "light" or idea. The world of absolute idealism—the belief that there must exist a meaning somewhere—is the illusory world, "the world as it isn't." The real world is the one appearing before us freighted with all its tragedy. The ultimate tragedy results when a surfeit of self-knowledge causes bewilderment. The purpose of light is to discern the darkness. Since possession of the light is sufficient to keep man from complete disaster, no illuminated life can result in failure. Those who have the light may still be darkened by "restlessness, longing and grief,"—but they are not desperate.

"Years are not life." With the passing of time Robinson steeled a faith that had somehow previously been securely concealed in doubt. The vision began to seek expression, not the bitterness of a man alone in time. He lived in hell—tormented at first by his inner light and later comforted by it. He was bitterly tortured and desperately unhappy, for poetry and companionship, which were all that mattered to him, seemed incompatible. Being a poet without readers was worse than being a Hamlet without his Horatio to report him and his cause aright to the

uninformed. Later, having gained relative security and acceptance and therefore partial peace, he was disturbed by love and
loneliness. A fuller peace came to him, however, from his disinterested loyalty to his art, in which he sublimated his love, his
duty, and his despair.

Robinson really went beyond Royce's philosophy of loyalty
to loyalty. The ultimate object of loyalty for him was truth.
Fearlessness in the face of the revelations of self-knowledge and
of dark omnipotence was to him the crowning human virtue and
peace, whatever its other consequences might be.

Stages of Robinson's Intellectual Growth

ROBINSON'S THINKING centers in four chief themes, which apparently occupied his mind successively, so that one can distinguish roughly four stages in his philosophical development. Even more significant than this is the fairly definite growth in perspective and analysis within each of these stages. The theme of tragedy remains constant in spite of the variation of subject, but Robinson's conception of the nature of tragedy deepens. Most of the poems written before 1916, notably *Captain Craig* and *The Man against the Sky*, are concerned with the tragedy of "light." Although the products of a later date, the poems of "the valley of the shadow," *The Man Who Died Twice*, and *Amaranth*, must be included in this group, for they, too, in a more mature form, reflect Robinson's transcendental skepticism with its emphasis on light in darkness.

Light and darkness, peace and fear, failure and destiny are the outstanding themes in these poems. Thus we have the peace of Captain Craig, who realizes his material failure, but is happy with his grim, laughing faith in a "laughing" God. The peace of Fernando Nash, in *The Man Who Died Twice*, is attained by losing his musical soul and finding a new, pathetic, satisfaction in "drumming for God" in the Salvation Army. Several characters, such as Pink, in *Amaranth*, turn to suicide, instead of to the peace of resignation. Fargo, in the same poem, illustrates most completely this philosophy of peace through despair. Few persons have peace, because of their unwillingness to admit defeat, their inability to recognize their shortcomings, or their lack of honesty in relinquishing false hopes. The many who never know peace are doomed through fear to suffer in the darkness which is unfolded when they achieve the sharp "light" of self-knowledge. While the light itself varies in kind, direction, and intensity, it is a mirror reflecting each one's own soul or lack of soul. In all cases the removal of fear and doubt leads to acceptance of destiny as the ruling force of the universe, despite any individual efforts to the contrary, so that resignation to these natural laws is *per se* a form of peace.

The earliest poems are dominated by the theories of the sentimental pessimists, by their interest in pathos, pity, and defeat. Robinson's disillusionment, fatalism, and skepticism are mingled from the start, with his humor, or sense of comedy, and with his idealistic loyalty to truth. Robinson constantly presents this idealistic faith in "light" as a contrast to the realism and mechanistic materialism of the age.

The poems of disillusionment gradually take on more austere forms of tragedy. Whereas the earlier and shorter poems, contained in *The Torrent and the Night Before, The Children of the Night,* and *The Town Down the River,* are brief character sketches or individual portraits reflecting romantic pessimism, the poems in *The Valley of the Shadow, The Three Taverns, The Man against the Sky,* and *Amaranth* increasingly show a more developed concept of tragedy. Instead of a Richard Cory possessed by disgust and self-pity, the man against the sky becomes human folly personified, universalized, and transformed by courage into the greater substance of Promethean tragedy. *The Man against the Sky* and *The Valley of the Shadow,* although more universal in theme than the earlier works, contain withal fewer details of experience than are embodied in the more recent *Amaranth* (1934). The tragedies of "light" culminate in *Amaranth*. Probably the experience gained during summers spent at the Peterborough colony is responsible for some of the characters in it and for the blending of comedy and tragedy.

The second period probably begins with reflections on Robinson's duties in New York and on the outbreak of the World War, when his leisure at Peterborough gave him a new perspective of the intricacies of human relationships. The tragedy of love in conflict with duty becomes the major theme and is portrayed in the Arthurian legends, *Merlin*, *Lancelot*, and *Tristram*. Although *Tristram* received the Pulitzer prize and achieved great popularity, Robinson himself considered *Merlin* the best of the three. These poems have a universality that *Captain Craig* and the earlier poems had, paradoxically, in a narrower sense. In *Merlin* the analysis is centered more in the personal conflict in Merlin than in the ruin of Arthur's kingdom. *Merlin*, the outstanding philosophical poem in the group, indicates Robinson's realistic reinterpretation of romanticism. Here we can note the poet's critical realism; he looks at life more objectively and timelessly, having overcome much of his earlier resentment. The elemental dualism of duty and love is given heroic and almost classic treatment. Keeping the political theme of the social duty of Arthur in the background as the imminent darkness or doom, the three poems stress the tragedy of variously involved love. It is important to observe that at this stage Robinson was primarily concerned with the tragedy of love and did not have a dominating interest in the social duties and tragedies of power. In 1932, in an inter-

[37]

view with Nancy Evans, Robinson remarked that *Merlin* expresses the full power of maturity, by which the Arthurian poems were to tell of "the breaking up of the old order." [1] As this conversation occurred many years after the poem was written, it is very probable that Robinson saw the seeds of his later social philosophy in these Arthurian poems, though the doom of Arthur's world was then still in the background of the poems.

The third group of poems is tangentially concerned with a similar topic, being the tragedy of marriage. The plays, *Van Zorn* (1914) and *The Porcupine* (1915), although of much earlier date, may be considered as introducing or foreshadowing *Cavender's House* (1929), *The Glory of the Nightingales* (1930), *Matthias at the Door* (1931), and *Talifer* (1933). The two plays belong to the class of later poems as far as theme is concerned, but treatment of the theme is comparatively meager. There is a particular relationship between the second and the third stages of Robinson's thinking. In both stages an interest in the tragedy of love is indicated; but whereas in the former this interest is in love's conflict with social duty, in the latter it is produced by its conflict with marital circumstances, conceived less as a bond of duty than as meaningless fate. In these poems the problem is created when incompatible people marry and the person most sincerely in love knows complete frustration. This situation, though a common one, was important in Robinson's own life.[2] Hence the poems are more intense, personal, subtle, and psychoanalytical than most uninformed, biographical critics are willing to admit. Nevertheless they are characterized by an amazing objectivity, an almost clinical analysis.

[1] Evans, "Record of an Interview," *The Bookman*, LXXV (November, 1932), 675–81.
[2] Carl Van Doren, *Three Worlds*, pp. 160–62.

In the plays *Van Zorn* and *The Porcupine* the heroes try to assist destiny, with varying results. In *Talifer*, too, the physician attempts this role, but less earnestly, manifesting a scientist's insight into the ways of life, and a humorous, reconciled regard for nature's methods and results. The dominant theme of this group, however, is not the "peace" of the scientist, but the tragedy of self-knowledge with regard to the failure of one's "house," home, marriage, or private concerns. The vision of Matthias is "not the cosmic vision; it is the personal vision, the inner truth of his own nature which is the persuasion by which a man lives." The wisest know, as does Timberlake, that "there is no cure for self."

The fourth and last stage shows Robinson thinking in social terms. Now the social note enters, with an analysis of the tragedy of "power." In *Demos and Dionysus*, *Dionysus in Doubt*, and *King Jasper* there is a social emphasis. *King Jasper* surpasses the earlier poems in universality and is a synthesis of all the periods, so that it includes the tragedy of light, the tragedy of duty, the tragedy of love—all culminating in the tragedy of power. The general sense of Robinson's social philosophy is contained in his foreword to Carty Ranck's *The Mountain*,[3] in which he discusses the romantic hatred of the Kentucky mountaineers toward one another.

it is seen to be yielding reluctantly a way for the inroads of education, compromise and prosaic common sense. Perhaps another age awaits us in which sense will become too common to be endured and in which we shall find ourselves engaged in reconsidering the example of a certain illustrious Monk of Siberia as an encouragement or an escape from the paralyzing conformities and enormities

---

[3] Ranck, *The Mountain*, with a foreword by Edwin Arlington Robinson, pp. 3–5.

of our quaintly alleged democracy, but the time is not today, nor will it be tomorrow, nor yet this year.

The Kentuckians could not understand the United States Government. "They wondered, somehow still a bit annoyed what difference it made to God, who provided so obviously and impartially for either product, whether a bucket of corn should be converted ultimately into meal or into whiskey." With similar keen ironic humor about drinking, these paragraphs reflect Robinson's social philosophy as expressed in *Dionysus in Doubt* and *Demos and Dionysus*—the liberty of an individual must not be impaired by a "miscalled Democracy."

Using Robinson's occasional figures, we may characterize each of these groups of poems in terms of his symbols for the tragic forces: first shadows, then castles, then houses, then chimneys. The shadows are the objects of his doctrine of "light"; the castles are the dark stage-settings for romantic passion and for Christendom and the Grail; the houses (of marriage) all have their dark "doors," which open usually into the "night"; the chimneys are the evils of power by which economic materialism defeats itself. However, regardless of period the theme of tragedy remains, and the problem of self-knowledge, with its transcendence of darkness, is forever present.

A glance over Robinson's life, with its concomitant concept of tragedy, points to a well-developed theory of reality and knowledge in the poems. The important factor in this evolution of tragedy is the varied stress on its source, which progressed as Robinson's thinking matured. Thus, while the tragedy remains uppermost, the emphasis shifts from light to duty, to love, and finally to a larger, all inclusive, more universal social tragedy.

Part Two : Philosophical Analyses

Light and Shadows

Captain Craig

IN THIS POEM, the first of the longer poems, Captain Craig, a Socratic itinerant, regrets his failure at lofty beggary more than the resulting cold and hunger. For this character Robinson had a living model, one Alfred H. Louis; and he used him to express "in verse—'impressionistic,' I fancy—the dim consciousness we have of things going forward." [1] For him life even fails to be a tragedy. Blaming no one for his condition, he considers his life a cause for joy, rather than regret. With his Tilbury townsmen Craig philosophizes on man's importance.

"Of all the many marvelous things that are,
  Nothing is there more marvelous than man,"
  Said Sophocles; and he lived long ago;
"And earth, unending ancient of the gods,
  He furrows; and the ploughs go back and forth,
  Turning the broken mould, year after year." [2]

Quoting Sophocles, he explains his own existence in similar fateful terms.

For Robinson the "music of the spheres" is a kind of laughter; although God's humor may be sardonic. This laughter is, not the cynic's sneer, but a genuine appreciation of the follies of human life. The theme of Craig's moralizing is that man must learn to laugh with God—the laughter of the wise as contrasted

[1] See Hagedorn, *Edwin Arlington Robinson*, pp. 132, 140, 168–69.
[2] Robinson, *Collected Poems*, 1934, pp. 117–18.

with that of the youthful cynic. Man must recognize the humor in the world which God sees and enjoys. Resignation to fate, not lamentation will be the result. It is important to note that humor comes only from wisdom, not from cynicism, for wisdom gives knowledge of the truth. This divine wise laughter is the "music of the spheres."

There is a positive joy in facing reality and laughing. Because art may alleviate man's unhappiness, it is the panacea of escape. Robinson here ridicules the pathos of his earlier sentimental pessimism, according to which life is completely evil, a state to be painfully resented rather than peacefully endured. This laughter, this sense of the farce, is a growing theme in Robinson's poetry. *Captain Craig* and *The Man Who Died Twice* furnish particular instances of that interpretation. It appears with the clarity of individual character analysis in *Amaranth* as well.

Craig knows himself to be a person who, seeing "the living light," is able to "read the sun," although he is a failure as far as the world is concerned. Ironically, Robinson seems to imply that unless one has enough power ostensibly to change the world, the world considers him unsuccessful, although the powerless man may possess enough light to be wiser and happier than the others. Craig is happy at being alive, for within him he feels "no dreariness, no grief, no discontent, no twinge of human envy." The latter categories of failure epitomize the types found in *The Valley of the Shadow*—the tired, the weary, the sorrowful, and the ambitious. Craig's attitude approaches Nietzsche:

> . . . Because one half of humankind
> Lives here in hell, shall not the other half
> Do any more than just for conscience' sake

> Be miserable? Is this the way for us
> To lead these creatures up to find the light,—
> Or to be drawn down surely to the dark
> Again? Which is it? What does the child say? [3]

Despite the shadow of futility, Craig believes an altruistic attitude to be a form of "light." Here appears the concept of duty
and service which is developed later in *The Glory of the Nightingales*. Nor does Craig believe that man's death terminates his
serviceability, for each has had some useful power by which he
has affected others. Robinson comments upon the cynic, who,
laughing at love, at beauty, and at the impermanence of the
things of daily life, is "shrewd, critical, facetious, insincere, and
for the most part harmless."

> What does he know about realities,
> Who sees the truth of things almost as well
> As Nero saw the Northern Lights? Good gracious!
> Can't you do something with him? . . .
> Is it better to be blinded by the lights,
> Or by the shadows? By the lights, you say?
> The shadows are all devils, and the lights
> Gleam guiding and eternal? Very good;
> But while you say so do not quite forget
> That sunshine has a devil of its own,
> And one that we, for the great craft of him,
> But vaguely recognize. The marvel is
> That this persuasive and especial devil,
> By grace of his extreme transparency,
> Precludes all common vision of him; yet
> There is one way to glimpse him and a way,

[3] Robinson, *Collected Poems*, 1934, pp. 126–27.

> As I believe, to test him,—granted once
> That we have ousted prejudice, which means
> That we have made magnanimous advance
> Through self-acquaintance. Not an easy thing
> For some of us; impossible, may be,
> For most of us . . .[4]

And so it is the devil in the light who leads us astray. Similarly, as shadows and light have devils, laughter is cynical and divine. The cynic really sees no devil in the light, because of "the great craft" of his transparency; he sees nothing there and is blinded by light. There is no wisdom in seeing through things; prejudice must be exorcised by a "magnanimous advance of self-acquaintance." The prerequisite of understanding is self-comprehension. This is a typical doctrine of idealism —that one must see things with the perspective of self-knowledge. Vision thus becomes relative and meaningful in terms of one's own individuality. Too few have the wisdom or the honesty of Craig's light, for

> . . . a man may learn
> That even courage may not make him glad
> For laughter when that laughter is itself
> The tribute of recriminating groans.
> Nor are the shapes of obsolescent creeds
> Much longer to flit near enough to make
> Men glad for living in a world like this;
> For wisdom, courage, knowledge, and the faith
> Which has the soul and is the soul of reason—
> These are the world's achievers. And the child—
> The child that is the saviour of all ages,
> The prophet and the poet, the crown-bearer,

[4] Robinson, *Collected Poems*, 1934, pp. 129–30.

Must yet with Love's unhonored fortitude,
Survive to cherish and attain for us
The candor and the generosity,
By leave of which we smile if we bring back
The first revealing flash that wakened us
When wisdom like a shaft of dungeon-light
Came searching down to find us.[5]

This quotation is an explicit statement of Robinson's idealism. The devil dwelling in the light is the temptation to see too far. Knowledge may sour to cynicism which throws vanity into grotesque relief. This insight gives Captain Craig an opportunity to sketch the various kinds of intelligence.

The poem is interwoven with an interesting "dream-vision" of the Fates, in which the subtlety of Robinson's thought is fully illuminated.

. . . Faint-hued
They seem, but with a faintness never fading,
Unblurred by gloom, unshattered by the sun,
Still with eternal color, colorless,
They move and they remain. The while I write
These very words I see them,—Atropos,
Lachesis, Clotho; and the last is laughing.
When Clotho laughs, Atropos rattles her shears;
But Clotho keeps on laughing just the same.
Some time when I have dreamed that Atropos
Has laughed, I'll tell you how the colors change—
The colors that are changeless, colorless.[6]

Lachesis is the past; Clotho the present; Atropos the future. According to the poem the past fades into the background

5 *Ibid.*, pp. 131–32.   6 *Ibid.*, p. 132.

while the present dares to laugh in the face of the future. The poet makes the subtle point that although Atropos may some day laugh (or the future seem bright); Robinson doubts whether the colors will change essentially. In short, who laughs with Clotho laughs with God. Time may seem changeful to us, the future may loom ominous, but even that is changeless; and while the laughter of the present rings, the future need not be feared. Is this not the old fear motif in a new setting? Fears do not keep us from laughing, for usually they are fears of a hypothetical situation, potential in the mind and nonexistent in our daily living.

Craig laments that he is a failure, having accomplished nothing in any particular field. Perhaps in his self-analysis Craig is Robinson speaking:

> But with a few good glimpses I have had
> Of heaven through the little holes in hell,
> I can half understand what price it is
> The poet pays, at one time and another,
> For those indemnifying interludes
> That are to be the kernel in what lives
> To shrine him when the new-born men come singing.[7]

Craig believes he has gleaned his light by living, although the walls of the world do not bear his coat of arms. He possesses too, a kind of happiness innate in the enjoyment of natural beauties and in the fact that he is a "free creature with a soul," knowing at times the "way of laughter on low roads."

In another dream Craig sees again the vision of the child and a laughing God. Seeing this child, the man, or the mystery, he sloughs off doubt and fear like a tattered garment. Craig, a

[7] Robinson, *Collected Poems*, 1934, pp. 133-34.

carpenter who has failed because his tools were unfitted for the task, is aided by the child, who redirects him by teaching him and encouraging him with regard to the importance of his own ability. In poems such as *The Man Who Died Twice* and *The Man against the Sky* individuals are looking for the "orient word," but the answer to their search is found less in hope than in innocent acceptance of present tasks and opportunities. The dream is another version of an earlier theme, in which man must find his own place and must be happy in knowing that he is fulfilling his duty by doing what he is best suited to do—which is to find one's own path leading to one's own light. The child is the light of innocence leading, not to a goal, but to confidence or peace. In the dream Craig asks of God, " 'But if I starve—what then?' said I.—He smiled." [8] This one light succinctly expresses Robinson's philosophy. Man is always worrying about the future, possessed with doubts, fears, and anxiety for his own welfare. He is always wondering about conclusions dependent upon events that have not yet occurred and which usually never take place. God looks down upon man and smiles at his folly. God laughs, but man does not—therein lies the tragedy.

Craig tells the story of a man who had a dream in which he heard a song with a triumphant theme that haunted him to distraction. Craig is glad that the man died young, for

> That measure would have chased him all his days,
> Defeated him, deposed him, wasted him,
> And shrewdly ruined him—though in that ruin
> There would have lived, as always it has lived,
> In ruin as in failure, the supreme

[8] *Ibid.*, p. 142.

Fulfilment unexpressed, the rhythm of God
That beats unheard through songs of shattered men
Who dream but cannot sound it.[9]

This music of the spheres, this laughter of the gods, is equally diffused for all, but unheard by many. These are the failures. It is their inability to catch the strains that makes them what they are. It is their vain attempts to achieve the impossible instead of the limits of their actual potentialities that precipitates defeat.

Craig's will epitomizes the idealist's philosophy.

. . . No man has ever done
The deed of humor that God promises,
But now and then we know tragedians
Reform, and in denial too divine
For sacrifice, too firm for ecstasy,
Record in letters, or in books they write,
What fragment of God's humor they have caught,
What earnest of its rhythm; and I believe
That I, in having somewhat recognized
The formal measure of it, have endured
The discord of infirmity no less
Through fortune than by failure. What men lose
Man gains; and what man gains reports itself
In losses we but vaguely deprecate,
So they be not for us;—and this is right,
Except that when the devil in the sun
Misguides us we go darkly where the shine
Misleads us, and we know not what we see:

9 Robinson, *Collected Poems*, 1934, p. 143.

We know not if we climb or if we fall;
And if we fly, we know not where we fly.

And here do I insert an urging clause
For climbers and up-fliers of all sorts,
Cliff-climbers and high-fliers: Phaethon,
Bellerophon, and Icarus did each
Go gloriously up, and each in turn
Did famously come down—as you have read
In poems and elsewhere; but other men
Have mounted where no fame has followed them,
And we have had no sight, no news of them,
And we have heard no crash. The crash may count,
Undoubtedly, and earth be fairer for it;
Yet none save creatures out of harmony
Have ever, in their fealty to the flesh,
Made crashing an ideal. It is the flesh
That ails us, for the spirit knows no qualm,
No failure, no down-falling: so climb high,
And having set your steps regard not much
The downward laughter clinging at your feet,
Nor overmuch the warning; only know,
As well as you know dawn from lantern-light,
That far above you, for you, and within you,
There burns and shines and lives, unwavering
And always yours, the truth. Take on yourself
But your sincerity, and you take on
Good promise for all climbing: fly for truth,
And hell shall have no storm to crush your flight,
No laughter to vex down your loyalty.[10]

---

[10] *Ibid.*, pp. 150–51.

Too many fear to climb lest they fall; but, although we have heard of many who having striven have fallen, we have also heard of those who have risen to the heights. Too many interpret a falling body for the falling spirit. The spirit of the climber knows no downs or failure, "so climb high." One must not be disturbed by the "dark laughter" that seems a warning; instead, climb ever upward to the light of truth. Faith and sincerity make for safe and successful laughter, despite the laughter of those below us. "Fly for truth" with "no laughter to vex down your loyalty."

This passage, with its emphasis on loyalty to the truth, seems purely Roycean; Robinson never comes closer to a preaching, or moralizing, attitude. He is preaching idealism, but idealism with a double meaning. The critic of loyalty must laugh at such idealism, while the idealist from the Robinsonian angle must see this laughter as an aid in his climb. Thus the laughter seems to be a criticism of the philosophy of loyalty as such; but it is not so according to the idealistic concepts of Robinson, for whom loyalty and its accompanying laughter are included in a larger perspective, in a larger concept of pessimism. The poem is a first attempt to come to terms with the romantic pessimism of his early poems; it is a Schopenhauerian form of idealism asserting itself against the early pessimism of the Schopenhauer and Hardy types, which were current at the beginning of the century. For Robinson human folly becomes a theme for the joys of wisdom, thus replacing the early, sentimental pessimism of other philosophers. With a Robinsonian attitude one can see the farce of human life instead of the pathos of human life; one can sit back and laugh instead of breaking down and weeping. The goal of life is implied by,

The truth we seek and equally the truth
We do not seek, but yet may not escape,
Was never found alone through flesh contempt
Or through flesh reverence. Look east and west
And we may read the story: where the light
Shone first the shade now darkens; where the shade
Clung first, the light fights westward—though the shade
Still feeds, and there is yet the Orient.

But there is this to be remembered always:
Whatever be the altitude you reach,
You do not rise alone; nor do you fall
But you drag others down to more or less
Than your preferred abasement. God forbid
That ever I should preach, and in my zeal
Forget that I was born an humorist . . .[11]

"There is yet the Orient," or there is yet the truth to be discovered or revealed by the light.

Again there is indication of the Roycean moralizing about loyalty when Robinson says that one does not rise nor fall alone, implying the duty of striving, if not for oneself, at least for mankind. Craig prefers being a humorist to being a preacher, which is really Robinson's own sentiment. However, underlying the humor there is a need to show why one should laugh rather than mourn, which is moralizing in a subtle form. What others call "love" and Craig calls "selfishness" is the root of all evil—the flower that keeps man from searching for the truth, which makes him unaware that the success or failure of others is dependent on his success or failure—on his climbing or falling. The following quotation restates how wisdom

[11] Robinson, *Collected Poems*, 1934, p. 153.

prevents defeat, how man must try to climb, and how man
cannot forget his fellow man.

> . . . Then did I turn
> My long-defeated face full to the world,
> And through the clouded warfare of it all
> Discern the light. Through dusk that hindered it,
> I found the truth, and for the first whole time
> Knew then that we were climbing. Not as one
> Who mounts along with his experience
> Bound on him like an Old Man of the Sea—
> Not as a moral pedant who drags chains
> Of his unearned ideals after him
> And always to the lead-like thud they make
> Attunes a cold inhospitable chant
> Of All Things Easy to the Non-Attached,—
> But as a man, a scarred man among men,
> I knew it, and I felt the strings of thought
> Between us to pull tight the while I strove;
> And if a curse came ringing now and then
> To my defended ears, how could I know
> The light that burned above me and within me,
> And at the same time put on cap-and-bells
> For such as yet were groping? [12]

> . . . When his eyes
> Have read the book of wisdom in the sun,
> And after dark deciphered it on earth,
> How shall he turn them back to scan some huge
> Blood-lettered protest of bewildered men
> That hunger while he feeds where they would starve
> And all absurdly perish? [13]

---

[12] Robinson, *Collected Poems*, 1934, pp. 155–56.   [13] *Ibid.*, p. 157.

. . . What you take
To be the cursedest mean thing that crawls
On earth is nearer to you than you know:
You may not ever crush him but you lose,
You may not ever shield him but you gain—
As he, with all his crookedness, gains with you.
Your preaching and your teaching, your achieving,
Your lifting up and your discovering,
Are more than often—more that you have dreamed—
The world-refracted evidence of what
Your dream denies. You cannot hide yourselves
In any multitude or solitude,
Or mask yourselves in any studied guise
Of hardness or of old humility,
But soon by some discriminating man—
Some humorist at large, like Socrates—
You get yourselves found out.[14]

It is characteristic of Craig that he wanted his friends to regard his death without regret and without fear. Humorous to
the end, he saw life as something to be laughed at; he wanted
his funeral music to be Handel, not Chopin. His music was
to be representative, loud, fearless, joyous, played with a brass
band and trombones. Trombones, indeed, and the onward
parade of life!

The Man against the Sky

As is his custom, Robinson differentiates the sources of light.
In this poem are the light of sunset and that of dawn. The light
seen by the solitary man against the sky is a fading or a dawn-
ing, depending upon his point of view. And the "man against
the sky" may be, not one man, but many men: (1) He may

have been able to endure a more steady vision of the light than his fellows, and so he may have seen beyond the grave into the future. (2) Innocent of the toil that produced his comfort, he may have lived calmly in the serene light of the present. (3) He may face the light of both present and future with cynical indifference. (4) The canker of a mean life bitterly hated may have brought him to the horizon's edge. (5) Confidence in his ability to interpret the meaning of scientific, mechanical knowledge with the devotion of a fanatic may have lured or guided him. To each of these types Robinson devotes a section of the poem, and he summarizes them in the lines:

> Whatever drove or lured or guided him,—
> 1) A vision answering a faith unshaken,
> 2) An easy trust assumed of easy trials,
> 3) A sick negation born of weak denials,
> 4) A crazed abhorrence of an old condition,
> 5) A blind attendance on a brief ambition,—
> Whatever stayed him or derided him,
> His way was even as ours;
> And we, with all our wounds and all our powers,
> Must each await alone at his own height
> Another darkness or another light . . .[15]

Although each man's path is different, all are of "self-dominion reft." Reason, light, or even mechanical science destroys the sense of independence. Hence it forbids both faith and suicide. Faith is in heaven and hell, or living in fear of hell and in want of heaven, which is no way to attain happiness. Similarly, oblivion through suicide is no way to attain peace, for this method

---

[15] Robinson, *Collected Poems*, 1934, p. 65.

is the oblivious "florescence of the diabolical." If we have not the "enormities" of faith and suicide, the "onward auguries" of thwarted will, though not precarious enough to rush into ruin, may yet feed on hope. Though we do not know where we are going, we do "of our transcience here make offering to an orient Word." In short, the man against the sky need not assume that he faces sunset, he may just as reasonably sacrifice himself to the dawn, for by sacrificing to the dawn he surrenders his transcience. Realizing he is ephemeral, he devotes himself, not to his own happiness, but sacrifices himself to the future or what he hopes will be a rising light. Time itself is thus a sacrifice to eternity. The real point is that to see beyond the sunset is not necessarily an illusion. Man need not think that his death is the end; rather his life, with its death, may be a contribution to a later dawn—a light for the future, but not for himself.

"Why pay we such a price?" Why sacrifice to the light? It would be "folly" if the sacrifice were to a nothingness where "all who know may drown." Superficially, if we know, we may as well drown; but if we do not want to do that, if we are not liars, we can see beyond the flood of nothingness. Although the faith in light is blind faith, not vision, it is, nevertheless, an act of will. There is no reason for braving life unless we have this faith. Robinson is laughing at faith in heaven and hell; he is laughing at faith in happiness and the fear of death or hell; but he does not laugh at faith in the dawn. Light points the way to the word, which may be a rising God or an eternally living word—he does not say. The tonic qualities of progress, the equality of death, science's "hollow toy, the Race," and the fear of death itself are insufficient reasons for living; but a blind faith in the ending of blindness is sufficient.

[57]

While *The Valley of the Shadow* is concerned with those who have already entered the valley, *The Man against the Sky* is concerned with those who are about to enter it. In short, it seems a prelude to a song of death. The man represents men of many kinds; the poem depicts their various attitudes in facing the end. An aloneness is the one quality they have in common; and as each climbs on alone, he sees a flame—a flame bright enough to kill the one who was,

> . . . alone up there
> To loom before the chaos and the glare
> As if he were the last god going home
> Unto his last desire.[16]

As each goes on his way, he goes toward his grave; yet variously they go. He may have taken "the bread that every man must eat alone; perhaps he went as one forsaken; perhaps he walked on courageously and stood, where others had fallen; perhaps he tried to mount higher than others had mounted before him; or, "he may have gone down easily" and with sure footing.

> Why question of his ease of who before him,
> In one place or another where they left
> Their names as far behind them as their bones,
> And yet by dint of slaughter toil and theft,
> And shrewdly sharpened stones,
> Carved hard the way for his ascendency
> Through deserts of lost years?
> Why trouble him now who sees and hears
> No more than what his innocence requires,
> And therefore to no other height aspires
> Than one at which he neither quails nor tires? [17]

[16] Robinson, *Collected Poems*, 1934, p. 60.   [17] *Ibid.*, pp. 61–62.

Perhaps it is best that he sees only the apparent; perhaps he will be rewarded for "seeing all things for the best." Another individual may have taken the light, not pessimistically but indifferently; he may have seen nothing in favor of good or of evil. Nothing may have mattered as long as he could not live to see the result. He may have been "a player without a part . . . a painter sick at heart with Nature's toiling for a new surprise," a cynic who saw little truth in a world where everything is "arrayed for doom," with "life a lighted highway to the tomb." He may have climbed so carelessly that ambition "his hopes to chaos led." It may have pained him to see his dreams destroyed by the flame, leaving no doubt to ease the certainty of failure. Perhaps "sick memories of a dead faith" disturbed him; perhaps the suffering of his friends makes his departure more difficult and confusing. The man who cannot overcome his memories "may struggle to the tomb unreconciled." Perhaps he prefers the agony of remaining on the hill,

> Or, seeing in death too small a thing to fear,
> He may go forward like a stoic Roman
> Where pangs and terrors in his pathway lie,—
> Or, seizing the swift logic of a woman,
> Curse God and die.[18]

He may have been more scientific in his approach, constructing "a living reason out of molecules . . . and one for smiling when he might have sighed had he seen far enough."

> Discovered an odd reason too for pride
> In being what he must have been by laws
> Infrangible and for no kind of cause.
> Deterred by no confusion or surprise

[18] *Ibid.*, pp. 63–64.

[59]

He may have seen with his mechanic eyes
A world without a meaning, and had room,
Alone amid magnificence and doom,
To build himself an airy monument
That should, or fail him in his vague intent,
Outlast an accidental universe—
To call it nothing worse—
Or, by the burrowing guile
Of Time disintegrated and effaced,
Like once-remembered mighty trees go down
To ruin . . .[19]

Robinson relieves the essential singleness of the tragedy with this further description of its varieties:

He may have been so great
That satraps would have shivered at his frown,
And all he prized alive may rule a state
No larger than a grave that holds a clown;
He may have been a master of his fate,
And of his atoms,—ready as another
In his emergence to exonerate
His father and his mother;
He may have been a captain of a host,
Self-eloquent and ripe for prodigies,
Doomed here to swell by dangerous degrees,
And then give up the ghost.
Nahum's great grasshoppers were such as these,
Sun-scattered and soon lost.[20]

Our "thwarted will" must admit its defeat rather than assert itself madly in the "enormities" of faith or of suicide.

[19] Robinson, *Collected Poems*, 1934, p. 64.   [20] *Ibid.*, pp. 64–65.

If, robbed of two fond old enormities,
Our being had no onward auguries,
What then were this great love of ours to say
For launching other lives to voyage again
A little farther into time and pain,
A little faster in a futile chase
For a kingdom and a power and a Race
That would have still in sight
A manifest end of ashes and eternal night?
Is this the music of the toys we shake
So loud,—as if there might be no mistake
Somewhere in our indomitable will?
Are we no greater than the noise we make
Along one blind atomic pilgrimage
Whereon by crass chance billeted we go
Because our brains and bones and cartilage
Will have it so?
If this we say, then let us all be still
About our share in it, and live and die
More quietly thereby.[21]

Robinson next raises the question of the man's destination.
No one knows; but we do know that we may "make offering
to an orient Word that will not be erased." No one has been
able to change the world, although "a few, by fate's economy
shall seem to move the world the way it goes." This is an oft-
repeated theme in the other poems—man cannot alter destiny.
Nor does he tell us why man should want to remain alive,
"when infant Science makes a pleasant face and waves again
that hollow toy, the Race." We do not know why man feels it
is better to live as long as possible despite the difficulties of life.

[21] *Ibid.*, p. 66.

In an early letter Robinson said the word we are all trying to spell is "God." He may mean the light. He certainly does not posit an anthropomorphic deity. An answer is suggested, or at least some possibility of a transcendent meaning, although we do not see it.

> Shall we, because Eternity records
> Too vast an answer for the time-born words
> We spell, whereof so many are dead that once
> In our capricious lexicons
> Were so alive and final, hear no more
> The Word itself . . .
> Are we in anguish or complacency,
> Not looking far enough ahead
> To see by what mad couriers we are led
> Along the roads of the ridiculous,
> To pity ourselves and laugh at faith
> And while we curse life bear it?
> And if we see the soul's dead end in death,
> Are we to fear it? . . .
> Why pay we such a price, and one we give
> So clamoringly, for each racked empty day
> That leads one more last human hope away . . .[22]

Is it possible to be alive and know the word, when few of those who did know it could know it without fear and terror? It is a paradox that makes men hate life, but fear death. Despite our experience and reflection, does everything result in nothingness?

> 'Twere sure but weaklings' vain distress
> To suffer dungeons where so many doors

[22] Robinson, *Collected Poems*, 1934, p. 68.

Will open on the cold eternal shores
That look sheer down
To the dark tideless floods of Nothingness
Where all who know may drown.[23]

The question remains—"Why live?" But it needs no answer, for it is rhetorical. There are "dark tideless floods of Nothingness," but there are roads where one may go into the light, as the stoic Roman went to death.

Robinson has repeatedly protested that this poem was not intended to suggest an ultimate skepticism and pessimism, though superficial readers usually see nothing more. To Hermann Hagedorn he wrote: "The world has been made what it is by upheavals, whether we like them or not. I've always told you it's a hell of a place. That's why I insist that it must mean something. My July work was a poem on this theme and I call it 'The Man against the Sky.'" [24] On another occasion he wrote:

I've been called a fatalist, a pessimist and an optimist so many times that I am beginning to believe that I must be all three . . . If a reader doesn't get from my books an impression that life is very much worth while, even though it may not seem always to be profitable or desirable, I can only say that he doesn't see what I am driving at.[25]

The Man Who Died Twice

Like many other characters created by Robinson, Fernando Nash is one tuned to music; but the chords are lost in him. They fill his head with notes of fire and plague him for cool peace; but there are none else to hear, for "all there was of music about the place was in a dusty box of orchestrations for the janitor." The lines "you had it once" and "I had it once" are recurring

[23] Ibid., p. 69.   [24] Hagedorn, Edwin Arlington Robinson, p. 302.
[25] Ibid., p. 286.

motifs of Nash's earlier inspiration and ambition for what most certainly was a lofty task. However, with the realization of his insufficiencies Nash loses his musical identity and lives in death as far as his musical life is concerned. It is important to notice that the doubts and fears of inability and failure cause the final catastrophe. He had worked on his scores for many years, but a "fog of doubt" was permitted to dampen a fire which if properly fanned would have evaporated its mists. Nash had not the strength or the courage to defeat his doubts, and so he was defeated by them. He had not the patience, the faith, or the intelligence to "wait for what is coming whether it comes or not." He has lost the complete faith—which he had once—in his own work. It is the loss of ego that identifies the death of his musical soul.

> And you had not the protest of a soul
> Between you and your right to stay alive . . .[26]

Had Nash retained his faith, he might have gained professional immortality, at least. Instead, he had been concerned with the wrong instruments—"the drums of death," which for him seemed more real than they should have seemed. He shows how much he regrets his poor judgment in this humorously tragic vein in which extreme despair, touched with lighter irony, affords the high relief.

> . . . Look at that burned out face of yours,
> You bloated greasy cinder, and say who.
> Say who's to care, and then say, if you will,
> Why anyone in a world where there's a cockroach,
> Should care for you. You insufficient phoenix
> That has to bake at last in his own ashes—

[26] Robinson, *The Man Who Died Twice*, 1924, p. 21.

You kicked out, half-hatched bird of paradise
That had to die before you broke your shell,—
Who cares what you would be if you had flown?
A bird that men are never to see flying,
Or to hear singing, will not hold them long
Away from less ethereal captivations;
Just as a fabulous and almighty fish
That never swam to sight will hardly be
For long the unsighted end of their pursuit.
Why do you make then such a large ado
Over such undefended evidence?
You fat and unsubstantial jelly-fish,
That even your native ocean has disowned
And thrown ashore, why should men ask or care
What else you would have been if you had waited?
You crapulous and overgrown sick lump
Of failure and premeditated ruin,
What do you think you are—one of God's jokes?
You slunk away from him, still adequate
For his immortal service, and you failed him;
And you knew all the while what you were doing.
You damned yourself while you were still alive.
You bulk of nothing, what do you say to that?
You paramount whale of lust and drunkenness,
You thing that was, what do you say to that? [27]

The tragedy of Nash's first life is that he is "a might have been." He might have attained the glory he and so many others have sought. In fact, Robinson makes us believe that he could have attained this glory if he had waited. Nash certainly is convinced that he would have done so. As a result, he turns from

[27] *Ibid.*, pp. 22–24.

earlier personal ambition to a pious penitence, with God the focus of his attentions and endeavor. With this shift there is a parallel substitution of self-abasement for pride. An "enamel of unrighteousness" coats him. He sees himself—

> The heir-apparent of a throne that's ashes,
> The king who lost his crown before he had it,
> And saw it melt in hell.[28]

In short, he had permitted himself too early a death. However, Nash is doomed to another life. The drums of death are quite ironically but valuably supplanted by the "drum for the Lord's glory." The Salvation Army claims his talents. Instead of a crown of personal glory or the golden glory of art, he could wear a crown of God's glory. He seeks redemption and finds it in prayer. He understands that while there was much behind him in life "there is always more if we go on." After his verbal self-abuse, Nash analyzes various methods of suicide which might be the best way out. Perhaps starvation would bring an answer from God, whom he had often offended, so that if he "lived again" he would not have the destructive shortcomings of his earlier existence. Suicide seems the only way to fuse his doubts for himself and his reverence for God. Nash had passed, and he continued to pass, his life in the "valley" having not yet seen the light.

Thus Nash devotes himself to remorse and recriminations and starvation. His state of hallucinations is excellently drawn in the images that follow. He bows to a picture of Bach.[29] He sees an orchestra of rats stream through the keyhole. Bach seems to nod a warning as the music approaches its climax. Throughout the presentation the drums of death which have so long plagued

---

[28] Robinson, *The Man Who Died Twice*, 1924, pp. 26–27.
[29] In Robinson's own room hung a picture of Beethoven.

Nash seem dominant. As subtly as the orchestra had appeared, it disappears, and Bach is again a picture. Nash doubts that the rats would have mocked him as they did if they had understood his hopelessness, remorse, and regret. His attempted suicide by means of starvation did bring change and surprise to Nash. His experience in the "valley" results in a sudden "clearness." Nash tries to deny this light, saying that it is but the brightness that precedes the darkness of night. Even peace may prove unwelcome. It is a favorite Robinsonian theme that although men strive for the happiness of peace, peace is precarious for most, even when, as rarely happens, it is attained. Nash's immediate reaction is varying. The calmness left him apathetic; but soon he was ashamed of his insults to God. Then, suddenly his joy "covered him like a sea of innocence, leaving him eager as a child." Martyrdom had purged him of fear and doubt, leaving a new peace—a peace without ambition and its attendant evils of frustration, defeat, and sorrow. Quite typically, Robinson describes Nash's state as a "new unwillingness not to live" with a "gratefulness of infinite freedom and humility." Robinson makes us feel that even the calm, which Nash had never dreamed of, was, as his previous suffering had been, a part of destiny. For Nash, with his new outlook, this peace has more value than any ambition or achievement. It is the light that enables him to know such peace. It is a light revealed after so many dark years in the "valley." But Nash is not prepared for peace. A new fear of peace overcomes him. He prays for death. Then, realizing that he is a fool to anticipate death that is not coming, Nash resigns himself to life and no longer fears the drums of death which had always seemed to beat for him. Nash, now out of "the valley of the shadow," returns to life, liberated and God-praising. Life seems a "singing light." The drums of death are dominated by the trumpets of life. What Nash had so long awaited was finally his. He can wait no longer. Overcome with praise and exhaustion, he craves God and life.

Mark Van Doren [30] explains Nash's first death as the death of his musical soul. Nash really had lost his whole soul by the first death, but his soul had been dominated by ambition rather than by music. Now he has peace, the opposite of ambition, also expressed musically. Though Nash has lost art, he has found life. Nash's drums are the drums of life. The other drums are "the last hop of the devil" as contrasted with the golden trumpets of God. We see Nash beating the drums of life as an evangel; and this new noise is the clamor for peace.

Robinson's humor again appears when Nash admits that both he and the Lord know his beating is just "noise." Nash's new piety, which has replaced his old ambition and almost-attained-success, is a certainty of uncertainty.

> . . . All we know about the world
> For certain is that it appears to be.
> And in so far as I am sure of that
> So am I sure that I was once as much
> As you believed and others feared I was.
> I have not drugged a clamoring vanity
> With lies that for a little while may seem
> To sweeten truth. There was no need of that;
> And God knows now that there is less than ever.
> Now I can beat my drum and let those drums
> Of death pound as they will.[31]

[30] Mark Van Doren, *Edwin Arlington Robinson*, p. 64.
[31] Robinson, *The Man Who Died Twice*, 1924, pp. 73-74.

We have in this quotation a sketch of Robinson's general philosophy. "The Lord's ways are strange"—but not to fear the inexplicability of life brings peace. It is a divine madness that bids us know good and evil; for we know the world only as "it appears to be." It is Nash's new zeal for service that saves him from insanity. He knows a new kind of wealth, attained from his fealty to the Lord. He believes that his fervor is a rare treasure surpassing everything else that he has lost or lacked. He has received life in exchange for his "soul."

> . . . God was good
> To give my soul to me before I died
> Entirely, and He was no more than just
> In taking all the rest away from me.
> I had it, and I knew it; and I failed Him.
> I did not wait.[32]

Nash's friend attempts to explain away Nash's life and errors by determinism and destiny, but Nash blames only himself for "losing what he had won too late." He does not want pity, for he is happy in being alive to praise God. He does not care what others think of him, for he believes he is doing the right thing. Robinson observes,

> To each his own credulity, I say,
> And ask as much. Fernando Nash is dead;
> And whether his allegiance to the Lord
> With a bass drum was earnest of thanksgiving,
> Confusion, penance, or the picturesque,
> Is not the story. There was in the man,
> With all his frailties and extravagances,

[32] *Ibid.*, p. 75.

The caste of an inviolable distinction
That was to break and vanish only in fire
When other fires that had so long consumed him
Could find no more to burn; and there was in him
A giant's privacy of lone communion
With older giants who had made a music
Whereof the world was not impossibly
Not the last note; and there was in him always,
Unqualified by guile and unsubdued
By failure and remorse, or by redemption,
The grim nostalgic passion of the great
For glory all but theirs. And more than these,
There was the nameless and authentic seal
Of power and of ordained accomplishment—
Which may not be infallibly forthcoming,
Yet in this instance came.[33]

Nash finds peace in the form of sublimated ambition. It seems to give him more pleasure than all his unsuccessful attempts at symphonic composition. His "inviolable distinction" is his ability to suffer as much as he had and still to retain a love for God. This distinction gives a "privacy" or an aloneness that all the more distinguished characters in Robinson have endured. Like all the others, he still is attracted to glory; but in his newer life it is a new kind of glory—the glory of God. Despite the apparent frustration there is "the nameless and authentic seal of power and ordained accomplishment"—his service to God. The authority of someone who has achieved something "distinguished," though privately so, is close to what Robinson calls happiness or success. But this happiness is ironical. Perhaps it is because he realizes that this destiny brings such joy that Nash

[33] Robinson, *The Man Who Died Twice*, 1924, 77–78.

develops such piety—a piety akin to that which Job achieved, when he worshiped God, not for his justice, but for his glory. Therefore Nash praises the Lord spontaneously for what he seems to be. Unlike the character of young Hebron in *King Jasper*, who rebels against the ways of destiny and attempts to direct them, Nash is resigned, complacent, even joyous. Robinson seems never to have stressed piety, since piety in a scene where destiny is acceptable is almost unnecessary. However, Nash's sincerity and his form of piety can be respected by the poet, for this piety culminates in peace.

Amaranth

Although *Amaranth* is concerned with the tragedy of light, its treatment differs from that of two earlier poems, *The Man against the Sky* and *The Valley of the Shadow*. For men against the sky the problem resolves itself to finding an alternative to either suicide or absolute faith. Similarly, in *The Valley of the Shadow* there are many people seeking a way out, but none attaining the desired goal. However, Fargo, in *Amaranth*, is at the same time the epitome and paragon of the valley folk. In this poem Robinson has weighed the problem afresh, and his insight is expressed in the delineation of Fargo's character. The poem is not an attempt to refute pessimism, but it throws new light on the problem by its analysis in terms of maladjustment. The fear complex, maladjustment, and lack of self-understanding are now considered more important than the "meaning of life" problem. Robinson now (as in *The Man Who Died Twice*) is more willing to see as comedy that which has previously appeared as pathos. *Amaranth* is a description of the search for peace or resignation after maladjustment. Fargo was enabled to see the comic side of his attempt to be a painter, when he should have been a plumber. Resignation to the menial and unartistic side of life is important.

In *The Valley of the Shadow* we find "pensioners of dreams," "debtors of illusions," and "those who saw too late the road they should have taken." In *Amaranth* there are likewise "the wretched, or the broken, or the weary, or the baffled, or the shamed," but they are seen in a new context—no longer in "the valley," but in the limbo of dark awakenings.

It is not clear from the text whether this poem is literally a dialogue in limbo or a nightmare [34] or merely a fantasy of Fargo's past, which he evokes as he gazes into the water. Perhaps it is the suggestion of his daemon—Amaranth. It is not of paramount importance to discover the literal prototype of the allegory, for regardless of interpretation the setting is the world of regrets and disillusionment—a world of memory.

Fargo, realizing that art's crucifix is not the burden for his back, stands at the wharf meditating death in the dark water as the only release from a misinhabited world. Upon hearing a voice suddenly remark that the other would be the wrong world, Fargo knows that "fear had found his heart," and turning sees what "might have been the eyes of death, if death were life." This voice has saved Fargo before; this time he needs more than a voice—he needs guidance, for,

> Only the reconciled or the unawakened
> Have resignation or ambition here . . .[35]

Amaranth, "the flower that never fades," admits he has no power beyond his singular recognition of destiny. In answer to Fargo's query he explains his fated mission to save—or, when feared, to destroy. Fargo follows, "For the same law that holds

[34] See Hagedorn, *Edwin Arlington Robinson*, p. 367.
[35] Robinson, *Amaranth*, 1934, p. 7.

[72]

the stars apart, holds you and me together." [36] Walking among the graves, Amaranth describes his effect upon various people: most pass without a smile; some see, curse, and die; others look, live, and are indifferent. These last are the reconciled, who neither live nor die.

The two now approach the Tavern of the Vanquished. The "long place was alive with nothing that was any longer there." [37] Inasmuch as the house seems vaguely familiar to Fargo, Amaranth explains that when he was there before his "zeal and ignorance" had stood between him and vision. There are many who cannot see; but if they insist on searching the mirrors in Amaranth's eyes, they will see.

Evensong, knowing he is not a musician and aware of dwelling in the wrong world, continues his unnecessary compositions because habit has "outlived revelation." We have evidence of Robinson's humor in his treatment of Evensong. Usually this humor is a blend of the sardonic with the irony of the situation. Nor is it an accident that the flute, suggestive of piping and the plaintive, should be Evensong's instrument. Evensong introduces the newcomer to the others at the tavern —studies in failure: Edward Figg, who sees backward, is a good man wasted as a lawyer; Doctor Styx, who cures aches that are not memories, should have been a ventriloquist. The case of the Reverend Pascal Flax is etched in acid: "He became a clergyman because he liked to talk and to be seen as one anointed for an elevation"; but, having lacked faith, he had no material for sermons, and he "left his flock to a new shepherd." His middle name implies that he may have been the sacrificial lamb to mammon. Robinson scorns "his crying conscience because he knew before he was informed." Younger men smile at Flax, not

[36] *Ibid.*, p. 8.   [37] *Ibid.*, p. 10.

realizing their environment; if they had realized it, they would hardly have felt condescension.

Likewise we smile at Pink, the poet, "who sits erect, impervious, and secure," and at Atlas, the painter, who used to be a stevedore. A glance at Robinson's life reveals more than a theoretical sympathy with the artist. Evensong asks Fargo not to pity the group, for should Amaranth let him go, he would join them. Here again we see Robinson's great antipathy for pity.

They discuss the past—its darkness and "dead roots." Flax, with a clergyman's point of view, does not think the roots are dead, for how otherwise would the trees survive the "stormy centuries." He, of the old school, wishes to be present should young Pink tear up the roots. The latter, positing his age as the age of art, grants himself eligibility for the job. Doctor Styx ventures the opinion that Pink is sick, not because of roots, but because of misgivings. Here again is emphasis on conscience and regret. For the lawyer the roots are something more immediate and personal; he lacks roots because he set out to grow in the wrong world, but being older he is now resigned to his misgivings. Pink, willing to "exist without the tonic of your sad example," longs for another world; while Atlas reluctantly has agreed, "and with a massive confidence that had no falterings, he longed away." Amaranth recommends that "in art, you must esteem yourself or perish."

The four older men have seen Amaranth and are reconciled to their failure; still, they fear him. Pink is not afraid to die; like the others, he feels he will survive the light and its revelations. After looking into Amaranth's eyes Pink is filled with "more surprise than terror." Unlike others who have adjusted themselves to the wrong world, he is unafraid and leaves it. Even this tragic moment is treated with blunt humor; for Pink says, "Excuse me, while I go and hang myself." Doctor Styx reviews the tragedy of each:

> For we are here by ways not on the chart
> Of time that we read once as ours to follow.
> Time here is all today and yesterday,
> For in the wrong world there is no tomorrow.
> We stayed and lingered, only to be lost
> In twilight while we saw where we were going;
> We slept and rested, and we slept again,
> Till we awoke where there was no returning.
> So let us drink to all we should have been,
> Telling ourselves again it is no matter;
> The more we lie, the more must we believe.
> *Similia similibus curantur.*[38]

Fargo leaves for the wharf—Amaranth follows. Later they return to the tavern, where they find the others viewing Pink's hanging body. In limbo Pink pokes fun at Atlas's art, with its "crude opulence of mortality." Atlas's change of profession is a loss to the stevedores. The humor becomes definitive when the lawyer, because Pink seems both dead and alive, is afraid to be an accessory to the crime. Pink begs that they be saviors and leave him where he is, which, though not heaven, has more law, more music, more divinity than Figg, Evensong, and Flax can imagine.

Once again Fargo and Amaranth are on the street, when the latter observes that those at the tavern, unable to reckon the hours, need him to tell them where they are and whether they are in the right world.

---

[38] Robinson, *Amaranth*, 1934, p. 22.

There are men so disordered and wrong sighted,
So blind with self, that freedom, when they have it,
Is only a new road, and not a long one,
To new imprisonment. But you, my brother,
You are not one of them. You caught yourself
Once in the coiling of a wrong ambition,
And had the quickness to writhe out of it.
You heard me, and you acted, and were free;
And you are here where now there is no freedom.[39]

The two now enter an old house, where they find Evensong, Amelia Watchman, and Ampersand, a large black cat which threw "a whispered hiss of hate at Amaranth." It is humorous that Amaranth, who taught others not to fear, "frowned as if he felt it." The introduction of Ampersand is truly a bit of inspiration. The subsequent action about the cat and its mistress is heightened by the subtlety and delicate balancing of Amaranth and Ampersand. When Watchman, the authoress who writes and writes and writes, with great bravado wishes to risk the self-revelation mirrored in Amaranth's eyes, Figg cautions; however, she insists on seeing Amaranth's eyes.

    . . . A thin scream came out of her,
And there was nothing more. She was not there.
Where she had been there was a little mound
Of lighter dust, and that was all there was.
"I think," said Evensong, "that she had always,
Hidden somewhere within her, unacknowledged,
A sort of love for me. With your permission,
I'll say she is mine, now." With careful hands
He put it all in a small envelope

39 Robinson, *Amaranth*, 1934, p. 34.

And sealed it with his ring. And then he said,
"If she had stayed, she might have learned too soon
Where she was living, and why she was here.
There was no resignation born within her.
Truth, coming first as an uncertainty,
Would have said death to her, and would have killed her
Slowly. Now I shall have her with me always." [40]

Her illusion is certainly tragic, but her abracadabra disappearance is comically heightened by Evensong's pride in final possession, which later culminates in a feeling of frustrated love.

They return to the tavern and find the others drinking and arguing as usual. Robinson's explicit humor sprouts again in the discussion of Atlas's picture, captioned "The Blue Horse." Figg's legal mind cannot comprehend such new language; Flax, still a clergyman at heart, begs for peace and good will. Ridiculing old sinners who think prayer can substitute for good works, he adds,

> . . . and nowadays
> Sinners in art believe there are short roads
> To glory without form.[41]

The wit here is double-edged. Is not Robinson sharing to some extent Flax's "old school" horror of all free art? The group cannot fathom a blue horse, especially since it exists in color without form. Styx amiably agrees with the others against a too-rebellious change, for "art has roots,"—however,

> The more I drink, the more I see a horse,
> And love him none the less for being blue.
> What do I see, if it is not a horse?
> If anyone says it's not, say Doctor Styx

[40] *Ibid.*, pp. 46–47.   [41] *Ibid.*, p. 66.

Challenges them to call it anything else.
I shall remain here neighing until I know
Why it is not. If it is not a horse,
What else, in God's name, is it? [42]

The others, preferring peace to controversy, decide to humor
Atlas; who has not desired pity, but rather has pitied the others
for comprehending their positions less than he comprehends
his. In order to keep the peace, Amaranth suggests leaving; but
Atlas insists upon looking into his eyes. Atlas slashes all his pictures as a result. To this Amaranth replies,

If you were not afraid of me, my friend,
Your faith would not have cared enough to look
Into my eyes—and you would not be here. [43]

At this moment Ampersand, "with a superior tread of ease
and ownership," arrives to see Fargo's picture; Fargo had hoped
that he had come to see him.

"Not so," said Ampersand, with a red yawn,
"I came to see the picture. Men go hungry,
And travel far, leaving their homes behind them
And their wives eating scraps, all to see pictures
That hungry men have painted. Art is cruel,
And so is nature; and if both are cruel,
What's left that isn't?" . . . "I don't like it."
Said Ampersand—who promptly caught a fly
And anxiously chewed air until he found it.
"Excuse me. He was flying to his fate,
And here was I, ordained to swallow him.
You call it nature's law. I, being a cat,
Call it a problematical free will.

[42] Robinson, *Amaranth*, 1934, pp. 67–68.   [43] *Ibid.*, p. 74.

If there's a difference, no philosophers,
I'm told, have caught it yet." [44]

The cat, assuming that Fargo realizes where he is, wonders why he has returned. Ampersand is content to be a cat, who, seeing a sparrow cannot choose; however, since men's instincts seem more flexible, they should manifest more freedom. Then why do men foolishly try to make their wishes their beliefs, and why is Fargo still painting? The sarcasm is brilliantly treated, and it reveals Robinson's conception of destiny as something other animals exhibit unquestionably, whereas man seeks vainly to deny it.

The scene shifts to Atlas's funeral, which Amaranth attends charitably, Evensong meekly, Fargo with no pity, for his way may be the same if he remains with the group. Among the graves Fargo feels there must be one that has been "waiting too long" for him. The sight of Atlas's grave starts the wheels of reminiscence and speculation in all present. Realizing that Evensong is "too dream-worn and indifferent to escape," Amaranth presents the choice of resignation or destruction. Unlike Pink and Atlas, Evensong chooses the resignation, but he is not deceived concerning the ultimate end that awaits him. Figg, who once wished he were dead, now doubts that Pink or Atlas "have achieved release"; yet he does not reproach them for their solution. Although he does not reprove the suicides because of their belated awakening in a wrong world, which "unassayed ambition said was right," their deaths shock him. While Evensong suffers from lack of incentive and Figg from indecision, Styx, indifferent, indolent, skeptically disinterested in the "moral torture and eternal doubt" of others, believes the answer is "time." Flax, the clergyman, describes himself as

[44] *Ibid.*, pp. 84–85.

fearing no God except the one living within him. Because this God has told him that each man has his own house, Flax cannot condemn Atlas, whose burden he could not feel. When he realized that as a minister he was "telling lies to friends that knew it," he fled from his own crumbling house. Remembering Pink's funeral, he suggests that they let him hang a while longer and that they do not vex him with their uninvited presence.

> There are complexities and reservations
> Where there are poets, for they are alone,
> Wherever they are . . . Though he fail, or die,
> The poet somehow has the best of us;
> He has a gauge for us that we have not.[45]

Amaranth insists that Pink has taught each of them some element of stinging truth. The doctor will think that death is the end; the preacher now is not certain as to what is evil; the lawyer will try to retain a glimmer of his own light. Amaranth hopes they will all live until they are not sorry they were born. Styx, with a scientist's doubt, will have to live longer than the others. Fargo admits that Amaranth's eyes no longer cause fear and that he is ready to leave the wrong world. Stronger for having obeyed Amaranth's voice, he is now certain that there is nothing to fear.

The company and the graves have disappeared, and Fargo is now alone with Amaranth and Evensong. It is well that Fargo, who now sees clearly, whereas before he did not see at all, has returned to gain certainty and its subsequent freedom from Amaranth, who says:

> . . . To a few
> I murmur not in vain: they fly from here

[45] Robinson, *Amaranth*, 1934, p. 99.

As you did, and I see no more of them
Where, far from this miasma of delusion
They know the best there is for man to know;
They know the peace of reason. To a few
I show myself; but only the resigned
And reconciled will own me as a friend.
And all this you have seen. You are not here
To stay with us; and you are wiser now
For your return. You will not come again.
Remember me . . . The name was Amaranth . . .
The flower . . . that never . . . fades . . .[46]

And Fargo saw him fade in a sudden lucent flood as,

The world around him flamed amazingly
With light that comforted and startled him
With joy, and with ineffable release . . .
Saw sunlight and deliverance, and all through him
Felt a slow gratitude that he was hearing
Outside, somewhere, at last, the sound of living—
Mixed with a quaint regret that he was seeing
The last of Amaranth and Evensong.[47]

For those who have read too cavalierly *The Man against
the Sky*, and consequently have dubbed Robinson a defeatist,
this poem affords ample refutation. In the scene describing the
sinking ship cargoed with the drunken, Ipswich beckoned
Fargo to the settling hulk with the promise of certain release.
But Amaranth held Fargo to life and dismissed suicide as no
solution whatsoever. The tone of the poem's final cadences
brightly bespeaks this. Such solicitude for the proper values in
life and for life itself marks a relatively positive interest in

[46] *Ibid.*, pp. 103–4.   [47] *Ibid.*, pp. 104–5.

skepticism and is a measure of Robinson's intellectual growth. When this poem was published, many critics were frankly baffled. For Robinson, sustaining his felicitous genius for structure, usage, and phrase-making, had created a fantasy of ideas. The poem was like nothing he had done before. The reviewers, weakly admitting their surprise, failed, on the whole, to realize the entirely fresh elements, excellently handled, which were embodied in this new poem. The figure of Amaranth was alternately considered "the genius of time itself," [48] "time's judgment on men's work," [49] and "reality itself, the spirit of timeless truth." [50]

Few possess the courage to seek the message in Amaranth's eyes. Failure and disillusionment are ever bitter draughts for the ambitious. Fargo, seeing this fearlessly, is cognizant of the humor of the situation underlying the individual tragedies. In the poem, whether a given career is comedy or tragedy depends upon the individual's reaction to Amaranth's

[48] Hillyer, "Amaranth," *The New England Quarterly*, VIII (March, 1935), pp. 113–14.

[49] Walton, "A Compelling Theme," *The Nation*, CXXXIX (October 17, 1934), 457–58.

[50] "A Modern Allegory," [Editorial], *The Times Literary Supplement*, London, No. 1722 (January 31, 1935), p. 58. ". . . The whole poem, in fact, is a sort of allegorical commentary upon the conditions of true being." Referring to the allusion of the gravediggers, "The humour, like the argument, is at times rather laboured. Mr. Robinson's circumlocutions are often an essential idiosyncrasy, but sometimes they are a clumsy habit.
As a whole, however, the poem presents the problem of the individual's adjustment to reality with sufficient point and droll ingenuity to keep the reader interested in Fargo's adventures among those who have failed to solve it. And while the spectacle of such failures, so elaborately unfolded, is hardly inspiriting except for those of a sardonic temper, Amaranth does encourage us toward the end to believe that a solution may be found even for the Figgs of the world who may all live
> Until you are all sure you are not sorry,
> Even here in the wrong world, that you are born;
while, as for Fargo, he ends by being freed from all fear of the Reality in which he had found his freedom."

truth. Pink and Atlas, respectively, are cases in point. Robinson mingles both elements successfully, not by alternating these moods of comedy and tragedy, but by fusing them.

According to Socrates in the *Symposium*, "the genius of comedy is the same with that of tragedy, and the true artist in tragedy is an artist in comedy also." That Robinson is such an artist is illustrated in this poem, where the subtle play of words and characters links tragedy to comedy inseparably. That he was conscious of this theme is reflected in many of his own comments, especially in his reference to "the difficulty (or possibly the vital advantage), of being born a comedian under the wrong (or again possibly the best) conditions." [51] The whole poem is most cleverly and artistically treated, being abundant in counterpoint of mood and idea.[52] It combines humor and tragedy in the comic manner of death and the witty conversations with the dead. The arguments against suicide still reveal Schopenhauer's influence and the problems of Robinson's youth, but the chief and serious concern has shifted to the problems suggested by Amaranth. In this study of the relation between life and art, the dead are not relieved of the fundamental problems of the living. The light of self-knowledge does not always bring happiness, since life without art is empty, though lived in "the right world," but usually it brings resignation. However, resignation does not always bear the seeds of peace. Certainly death is not peace. According to Amaranth, "Death is death."

This light is revealed or reflected by Amaranth, who, not a power in himself, but a product of a greater force, is light as distinguished from the power whence it derives. His influence

[51] Hagedorn, *Edwin Arlington Robinson*, pp. 179–80.
[52] The poem probably reflects a great deal of Robinson's own attitudes and temperament.

on others as a light which gives them power to resign themselves either to life or to death, depending on individual merit,
is as presented by Robinson a method of dealing with maladjustment. It is important to observe that whereas Amaranth has
great control over others, he has no power over himself; and
being directed by destiny, he cannot decide whether a man
should see the truth or not. If he could, he would bar many
from revelation and consequent suicide. In short, Amaranth
merely grants self-vision. In solitude, when particularly conscious of his failures, each character searches his own nature.
Robinson treats this philosophic wonder in his characteristic
manner—by repeating the question and so adding to its clarity
step by step. Although there is no answer, men nevertheless
ask, or at least they cannot help wondering. This is the difference between poetry and science; where science shuns unan-
swerable questions, philosophy gravely wonders. Thus the
characters in "Amaranth" speculate when alone, but at well-
timed intervals, when each hears the tinkling bells that recall
him to society or to the group, he assumes a comic attitude intended to betray an underlying doubt. Each character is influenced either by Amaranth, who reveals reality, or by the other
allegorical figure, Evensong, who represents the remembered
events of life. The personal success of each depends upon
whether, having taken advantage of the light that Amaranth
reveals, he changes his world or, as Evensong implies, continues
his old song of darkness, of evening, of death. Evensong
seems to be a repetition of the past without change and without light—an even song. He sings of the end, implying death,
whereas Amaranth, "a flower that will not fade," remains forever.

Although at that time many critics believed that Robinson

had lost his grip on himself,[53] actually he showed philosophical development. *Amaranth*, presented as a mirror with powers of reflection, is an important contribution to the doctrine of light. Robinson seems to have attained a new perspective on light. The problem of self-revelation accomplished by light is no longer meaningless. The poem is a new statement and a more detailed analysis of the implications of self-knowledge.[54] Despair evades the problem, while resignation to oneself through psychological analysis becomes more important. The other characters have failed to find their proper vocations, whereas Fargo, by contrast and through self-understanding, has found his. Freedom consists in proper adjustment by ridding oneself of self-deceit, wrong ambition, and beguiling delusions. Only by the practice of such resignation can one attain the peace enjoyed by "A foe to phantoms, and a man attuned to his necessities."

[53] See Hillyer, "Amaranth," *The New England Quarterly*, VIII (March, 1935), pp. 113–14.
"Those readers who have of recent years been somewhat disappointed in Mr. Robinson's work will welcome this rejuvenation of his powers. I should go so far as to say that he has never surpassed Amaranth." This is not necessarily favorable.

[54] Walton, "Defeated Aspirations," *New York Herald Tribune Books*, October 7, 1934, p. 21.
"Is there a more subtle undercurrent here in Robinson's design? Does he believe the great artist will know himself as dedicated to his purpose, that only those who would fool themselves about their real usefulness must dwell in limbo resigned, or, unresigned, the veil stripped from their eyes, must kill themselves? Perhaps this underlying theme is here. In all this array of characters (abstractions drawn from any group of would-be artists) there is not one single genius. For the small person art, a profession, a delusion of grandeur, can be a mere escape from life. Only the great artist looks steadily at reality and at himself and creates. Amaranth is the desire within men toward immortality, toward fame. But his eyes speak the ultimate judgment of Time upon all men and their works." Robinson himself banked everything on writing unfading poetry and therefore took a chance. Doubt as to whether he should devote himself to poetry haunted him, but he had a fairly early resignation to his work and intended to stake everything on it.

Love and Castles

Merlin

With the exception of *Captain Craig*, which is somewhat shorter, *Merlin* is the first of Robinson's long poems. Like those which follow, it indicates the poet's interest in the effects of time on the individual's growth and perspective. The religious language of faith focuses the action on the Grail and presents a parallel rather than a contrast to his interest in science, which is frequently represented by characters who are physicians. In both situations, since neither religion nor science gives the answer to the problems of life, the characters speculate and wonder.

Despite the obvious medieval background, critics have seen the World War working in the poem. Mark Van Doren remarks,

Critics have pointed out that certain passages in "Merlin" and "Lancelot" are pertinent to the recent war, and have suggested that the poems by intention are commentary upon a contemporary system in ruins. But this is to underestimate the scope of their reference, which surely is to universal issues. Mr. Robinson, starting from Camelot, has attached his imagination to the farthest walls of the human world.[1]

While Van Doren does not refute the possibility that the poem is a generalized reflection based on a contemporary problem, he justly claims that the issues can be—and are in this case—

[1] Mark Van Doren, *Edwin Arlington Robinson*, p. 67.

both contemporary and universal. In fact, their universality is enhanced and clarified by their existence at the present moment, in past history, and probably in the future. Robinson's use of contrast, chiaroscuro, and sharp antithesis of extreme cases, are so peculiar to him that the medieval trappings of what is a scene of war give semblance of eternity to both the past and the present.

Several new figures in the poem, such as the dragon, the "specks," and the light of Galahad, are obscurely treated, yet they have a bearing on the growth of Robinson's philosophic themes, and his wider concern with love, duty, and government. King Arthur has founded his kingdom on sin. Arthur's "two pits of sin" are his taking as queen a woman who is in love with his favorite knight and his complete neglect of duty to his people while rapt in somewhat uxorious enthusiasm for that unfaithful wife. The dragon—a living sin, subsisting on prevalent error—could not be destroyed until kings and their wayward kingdoms were destroyed. Arthur has abandoned the world of duty for love.

The profound relationship between love and duty is illustrated in the philosophy of love built by Merlin and Vivian and the philosophy of duty recognized belatedly by Merlin and Arthur. Merlin's early attitude was one of duty to sovereignty—a duty which made him select Arthur as ruler and then warn him that he would be doomed unless he forsook the ways of sin and discerned through his enveloping veil of love the waiting dragons. After fulfilling this duty Merlin turns to a warmer kind of personal happiness; he turns to Vivian's love. However, so deeply rooted is his original devotion to his king, that at the latter's command he leaves Vivian's magic to return to Camelot's doom. This solution of love and duty in the alem-

bic of Merlin's unique prescience makes for his doom, as it
makes for Arthur's. The king, to be sure, mingles the same in-
gredients, not in wisdom, but in the darker passion of a mood.
Hence Merlin's pity; for it is the direct result of his prognosti-
cation. Since no one can separate Lancelot and Guinevere, and
since war is imminent, Arthur must not waste his time in emo-
tional wonderment or in vain faith in his divine security.
Whether or not his hate overbalances his force and vision, passion will cost him his kingdom. It is strange that Arthur, ostensibly oblivious of all the apparent intrigue in his palace,
does understand that because he has founded his kingdom on
sand and mud he will not see the Grail.

> "Nor I," said Merlin. "Once I dreamed of it,
> But I was buried. I shall see no Grail,
> Nor would I have it otherwise. I saw
> Too much, and that was never good for man.
> The man who goes alone too far goes mad—
> In one way or another. God knew best,
> And he knows what is coming yet for me.
> I do not ask. Like you, I have enough." [2]

We see Arthur suffering from too little light, and Merlin
from too much. Merlin indicates his resignation by not ques-
tioning the future, although he sees into it. Arthur, surrounded

[2] Robinson, *Collected Poems*, 1934, p. 254. According to Mark Van Doren:
"Mr. Robinson has been deeply concerned with men who see too much;
he finds them as pitiable as those men who see too little, or see not at all.
This does not mean simply that Mr. Robinson cries out for us to beware
of the pride that goeth before a fall, or that he deprecates fanaticism, or
that he meets inspiration with cynicism. It is rather that in his passionate
skepticism he refuses to agree that any one vision is the universally valid
one, that in his view of the battle which silently goes on in the world
between darkness and dawn there can never be a decision for man—for any
one man at least—to render." Mark Van Doren, *Edwin Arlington Robinson*,
p. 57.

by the "loneliness of kings" and "intolerable doubt," goes to darkness from even his little light. Lying awake, Arthur sees "giants rising in the dark, born horribly of memories and new fears," and realizes the truth of Merlin's warning. He is further disturbed by his overestimation of Vivian's active hold over Merlin. In this respect they are mutually distrustful of one another. The woman sees bleak duty keeping her lover from fire and youth; the king sees his minister kept inextricably by a woman's love. It is perhaps noteworthy that while Lancelot and Arthur are never released from passion, Merlin leaves his love, scarred as were neither king nor knight; he alone survives their world, but his wounds are more horrible than those inflicted by war and swords.

Arthur's sin lives in the dragon; forgetting his kingship, he thinks only of Guinevere's love. Merlin's wisdom edges his memory to sharp remembrance. The doom that follows reveals the moral reign prescribed by God for men and kings. But they, abandoning the moral laws to serve passion with fealty, must face the dragons of doom. Thus we see Arthur doomed; the problem being one of personal happiness as opposed to group welfare. The king must realize that his duty to the state cannot permit interfering personal love to flourish. Another evidence of the inconsistency or incompatibility of love and duty is evidenced by Vivian's indifference, in fact boredom, at Merlin's references to pits, dragons, and sin. For her they are unknown categories, meaningless in the lexicon of love. His world parts from hers at this point: both see love and duty to be mutually exclusive. For Vivian duty to the king is made of reason, not passion.

Robinson presents the contrast between morality, considered as duty, and love, as personal indulgence. Love is escape from a situation where duty is permanent. An attempt to compromise duty with love leads to failure and defeat. Merlin tries to escape to Broceliande, but is only temporarily successful. Realizing the impossibility of permanent love, he becomes resigned to his fate; while Arthur, with no effort to reconcile his duty, provokes not only his own downfall but also the complete undoing of the state. If he had remained faithful to his rule, he would not have been doomed or loved.

Similarly, Merlin's attempted synthesis of love and duty proves a failure. When he sees that Vivian cannot consider his allegiance to Arthur, he feels a sudden "melancholy wave of revelation." He becomes a victim of change—"a mightier will than his or Vivian's." Change has spotted certain people. They are speckled, not with the flaws of human nature, but with the characteristics which affect the lives of others. Arthur is a "speckled king" whose command alters Merlin's life with Vivian. Merlin, always boasting that he feared no "specks," asserts that he would fear more if he were king of Camelot. The specks represent the scars caused by remissness in the performance of duty. Arthur was speckled by the sins of neglected duties and improper love. He fears not specks or a doom greater than specks—doom which Merlin would have feared, because he realizes its inevitability under such evil circumstances. In fact, Merlin does not think in terms of specks; but Vivian, a creature above all earthly problems, a figure of love completely removed from duty, sees duty and the objects of duty as specks that mar one's happiness and therefore to be feared by others. All, including Arthur, the queen, Modred, and Lancelot, seem speckled to Vivian. Each has sinned against the other either by illicit love, breach of duty, deceit, or envy. Each is blemished as a result. Vivian's disrespect for Merlin's

beloved king, her absolute misunderstanding of a duty which
is so vital to Merlin, makes him more aware of change, more
completely alone. These favorite themes of seeing too far
and seeing alone are illustrated by,

> . . . "The man who sees
> May see too far, and he may see too late
> The path he takes unseen," he told himself
> When he found thought again. "The man who sees
> May go on seeing till the immortal flame
> That lights and lures him folds him in its heart,
> And leaves of what there was of him to die
> An item of inhospitable dust
> That love and hate alike must hide away;
> Or there may still be charted for his feet
> A dimmer faring, where the touch of time
> Were like the passing of a twilight moth
> From flower to flower into oblivion,
> If there were not somewhere a barren end
> Of moths and flowers, and glimmering far away
> Beyond a desert where the flowerless days
> Are told in slow defeats and agonies,
> The guiding of a nameless light that once
> Had made him see too much—and has by now
> Revealed in death, to the undying child
> Of Lancelot, the Grail. For this pure light
> Has many rays to throw, for many men
> To follow; and the wise are not all pure,
> Nor are the pure all wise who follow it.
> There are more rays than men. But let the man
> Who saw too much, and was to drive himself
> From paradise, play too lightly or too long

Among the moths and flowers, he finds at last
There is a dim way out; and he shall grope
Where pleasant shadows lead him to the plain
That has no shadow save his own behind him.
And there, with no complaint, nor much regret,
Shall he plod on, with death between him now
And the far light that guides him, till he falls
And has an empty thought of empty rest;
Then Fate will put a mattock in his hands
And lash him while he digs himself the grave
That is to be the pallet and the shroud
Of his poor blundering bones. The man who saw
Too much must have an eye to see at last
Where Fate has marked the clay; and he shall delve,
Although his hand may slacken, and his knees
May rock without a method as he toils;
For there's a delving that is to be done—
If not for God, for man. I see the light,
But I shall fall before I come to it;
For I am old. I was young yesterday.
Time's hand that I have held away so long
Grips hard now on my shoulder. Time has won." [3]

Merlin had seen too far in Arthur's estimation, but he could not see the path that he himself had taken. If he had known Vivian before he knew Arthur and his duty to him, he might have known only love and had no conflict. Not seeing the light, not taking the morally chosen path, even as Merlin, Arthur, Modred, Lancelot each did not, results in "defeats and agonies." Just as Arthur was doomed for not seeing enough, Merlin suffered loneliness and defeat for seeing too

[3] Robinson, *Collected Poems*, 1934, pp. 294-95.

much. He saw so far that he could not think of his own existence as separated from a loyalty to Arthur. Merlin's doomed unhappiness lay in seeing alone. His fate was loneliness. Knowing what he did, he could not remain in the all-too-human paradise of Broceliande. He had to follow his light although aware that unlike one who was fortunate to find the pure light of the Grail, his was a distant light, never to be reached, but bright enough to show him where he had failed. Time and change had deprived him of his goal, but he had had enough light to realize that each man is a groping, swollen will vainly attempting to direct the world.

To Merlin the end means more beginnings.

> . . . It was the end
> Of Arthur's insubstantial majesty
> When to him and his knights the Grail foreshowed
> The quest of life that was to be the death
> Of many, and the slow discouraging
> Of many more.[4]

Of all who had seen the light, only Galahad remained calm. His was a light by which men saw themselves mirrored in one another. Gawaine was willing to die for the Grail, but was ineligible and returned to new iniquity. Lancelot returned as one who saw more than he should have seen; he did not find perennial joy in the queen. Some found life unnecessary. "They all saw Something. God knows the meaning or the end of it." Dagonet believes that Merlin can cure the king and end the upheaval. Merlin replies:

> . . . All this that was to be
> Might show to man how vain it were to wreck

---

[4] *Ibid.,* p. 305.

The world for self if it were all in vain.
When I began with Arthur I could see
In each bewildered man who dots the earth
A moment with his days a groping thought
Of an eternal will, strangely endowed
With merciful illusions whereby self
Becomes the will itself and each man swells
In fond accordance with his agency.
Now Arthur, Modred, Lancelot, and Gawaine
Are swollen thoughts of this eternal will
Which have no other way to find the way
That leads them on to their inheritance
Than by the time-infuriating flame
Of a wrecked empire, lighted by the torch
Of woman, who, together with the light
That Galahad found, is yet to light the world.[5]

Robinson questions those who have attempted to save the world by the love of woman and the love of the Grail. The two lights of which Merlin speaks are sexual love and the love of God. These two lights of the world form one of Robinson's essential themes. Similarly, there are two objects of love— woman and duty. The world is not saved by love alone. On the contrary, love here is an escape from the world. There are "two fires that are to light the world"—woman and the Grail, for even stronger than love is duty. For Robinson the only way to get over the swollen self-conceit that haunts us all, whether in self-love or in love of others, is through moral devotion—a devotion to duty. It is the expression of the free will of each individual. In this respect Robinson's concept of duty as a swollen will is Schopenhauerian and out of sympathy

---

[5] Robinson, *Collected Poems*, 1934, p. 307.

with the Christian philosophy of will which is swollen love. Likewise, in respect to duty Robinson reflects Royce's attitude toward loyalty, in which duty is essentially noble and stabilizing.

Royce attempted the Christian reconciliation—making loyalty itself an object of love in the sense of "devotion." He used loyalty instead of duty precisely in order to reconcile it with love. The light of the Grail probably represents the attempt to reconcile the light of duty with the light of love. The two lights are eternal sources of tragedy; their social reconciliation, reciprocal self-knowledge, is merely pathetic.

In the earlier poems love is in the foreground. The later poems stress duty in its various forms. Both have many parallels. Merlin is to Arthur what Honoria [6] is to Jasper—a prophet of impending doom. Both seers saw too much for their own happiness; both rulers saw too little—Arthur seeing not at all, Jasper seeing too late. Arthur thought only in terms of love, never of duty. Jasper felt the pangs of conscience and at least realized that he had been wrong to neglect his civic duties. Both poems have women (Vivian and Zoë) who symbolize pure light; but whereas Vivian represents the light of love, Zoë stands for the light of reason. In short, though the themes of kingship, love, and duty are similarly treated in both poems, in the later poem there is development toward a moral devotion which surpasses love. The two lights of Merlin have become one flame in King Jasper.

[6] See analysis of *King Jasper*.

Love and Houses

Cavender's House

THE POEM, a study in doubt and fear, is in direct contrast with *The Glory of the Nightingales*, in which the characters are intellectually fearless. Here man's fear is primarily one of himself—of his own motives. Cavender does not possess the light, but his wife reveals it—that is, the truth. The ghost is the truth. She is the answer to his doubts; and his doubts are his fears. The essential theme, then, is the difficulty of seeing oneself in the dark glass of doubt. An analysis of the succession of Cavender's problems and Laramie's answers will indicate Robinson's attempt to drive home the fact that since there is no point in starting with doubt, one should begin with facts. Revealing the futility of regret, remorse, and moralizing, the philosophical analysis centers in self-recrimination, self-accusation, and fatalism.

Having murdered his wife, Cavender attempts to convey the source of guilt away from himself; but his attempt is futile, because the sources of action can always be traced to objective situations or facts. Cavender, marked with a "scar that will not heal," has ruined his own existence by ending his wife's. Whereas she has a key to peace, Cavender is in a doorless hell of misgiving and wonder—"an eternity in time." He is haunted by memory, which stands between him and peace, rendered more painful by dint of his ignorance of any possible justification for his act. Such contemplation of a hopeless, irrevocable predicament is tragic. His memory is now the underlying cause of the tragedy, although the original drama was precipitated by his doubts.

After Cavender had killed his wife, he was doomed to a living death, which no amount of reminiscing or self-accusation could alter. Giving himself up to the law would bring peace, for the revelatory nature of a public expiation would be more satisfying than a secret demise. Cavender's peace must be alloyed with punishment. And in his catalogue of doubts is this dread of a guilty, nonsacrificial peace; looming behind this is the vast, evil jinn of his past. Surging qualms of conscience prevent him from finding oblivion and the clarity of self-comprehension. "If I had done so and so," is his recurring thought, but always the same answer is returned. "You should have known."

The transition in Cavender's fears occurs at the time of his entrance into the house. He does not fear death, but he does fear the possibility that others may learn his secret. He shuns, not eventual discovery, but immediate apprehension, which would prevent his meeting Laramie's ghost. His horror is "conceived of doubt more than of terror." And thus, overcome by suspense, which was more upsetting than the impact of certain knowledge, Cavender seeks an answer to his questions. His doubts darkly adumbrate the mute inhabitants of the house: the pictures, chairs, and associations which even the bared walls have not relinquished. It is while feeling the unseen light of Laramie's ghost that he hesitates to look up, "for doubt of what was there." Again in her eyes he sees "an evil and an innocence."

> . . . Tonight,
> If his remorse achieved humility,

They might reveal a reason, or show none
To be revealed, for longer fearing them,
Or fearing not to know.[1]

There is a long silence before Laramie answers him. There are no new fears for him, but she cannot tell him how to endure life after he has wrecked it so. His skepticism as to her presence is transformed into anxiety lest she should disappear. Laramie, ambiguous in reply, urges him at length to forget his deed and blame destiny for his action. For Cavender is a part of nature. Beyond that she cannot help him, nor can she show him the irenic light of her quietude—for he is alive. It is interesting to note that her faith in fate is the kind of belief that holds Robinson's respect. Perhaps Cavender will "survive his memories" and be happy again or, at least, peacefully alive.

In the conversation Cavender is heard to speculate on the existence of God, of purpose in the universe, and of the meaning of various phenomena. Her mercy consists in the negative but encouraging lack of certainty concerning his perpetual torment. Cavender wavers between mistrust of her presence and of her solace. It is typical of his mental state that he does not dare to take her hand, fearing his seizure will result in irrevocable silence. In this section of the poem he is never on friendly or trusted ground.

If she was there to lacerate him, she
Could only be God's agent in the matter—
And so there must be God; or if not God,
A purpose or a law. Or was the world,
And the strange parasites infesting it,
Serpent or man or limpet, or what not,

[1] Robinson, *Cavender's House*, 1929, pp. 12–13.

Merely a seeming-endless incident
Of doom? If it was so, why was it so?
He could do nothing. He was in a trap.
Nothing was on his side.[2]

We see here a slight change of attitude. His earlier doubts
tended to be less ambiguous when her infidelity was involved;
he now wonders whether or not the whole tragedy was pre-
ordained. Laramie hints that by taking fate into his own
hands or by attempting to do so, he has made his own road
darker. For, had he waited, he might have known and been
free. He is, however, perplexed, that coming as she has, she
offers no completely satisfying answer. It seems a "part of
her to have no reasons." Laramie suggests that he give himself up to the law; thus he, "would not have so long a death."
The admission that she has not yet found justice, but hope,
leaves Cavender imploring for the truth. Was her infidelity
actual or imagined; was his act beyond any mitigating circumstance willful and brutally unforgivable? Again he waives
her powers of forgiveness in a demand for an answer. But
Laramie says:

Your living and my dying, for example,
Are nothing to your knowing whether or not
My freedom was a sin. Why do you ask,
I wonder.[3]

The situation here resembles the conversation between Malory and Agatha in *The Glory of the Nightingales*. The living
are convinced by some ineffable and illogical thought that the
departed have found an answer to the meaning of life. Robinson maintains that although they have not found the single

[2] *Ibid.*, p. 47.   [3] *Ibid.*, pp. 66–67.

answer, they have acquired peace and resignation—without knowledge. Fear among the living is bred of ignorance and error. The living who dwell in darkness know their darkness, which is the *corpus* of truth. Laramie believes he is miserable because he has killed her. Knowledge of the causal facts would not alleviate his condition, for "knowledge is cruel."

> . . . There are those laws
> And purposes of yours, always at work,
> And doing the Lord knows what with our intentions.
> Eternity may have time and room to show us
> How so transformed a fabric may be woven
> Of crimes, corruptions, and futilities,
> That we shall be confounded with a wonder
> At our not seeing it here. Yes, there is hope . . .[4]

Still Cavender lacks "the balm of certainty to wash his scar." It would have saved him from always asking an unanswered question. The problem of her sin, his cause for doubt, essentially symbolizes the quest for the meaning of life. With pity and love and without a key of revelation, she recommends that he choose instead of death, hope, which is "real but uncertain."

Laramie questions his fear of dying. Perhaps her death has now removed his fear. For a brief moment Cavender thinks that she has come to his assistance, with these words:

> . . . You are afraid
> Of time and life, and you are afraid of me;
> But you are not afraid of dying, so long
> As you shall have a mortal right to die.

[4] Robinson, *Cavender's House*, 1929, pp. 74-75.

Cavender, you are no such fool as that.
There are still doors in your house that are locked;
And there is only you to open them,
For what they may reveal. There may be still
Some riches hidden there, and even for you . . .[5]

The doors are metaphors for the new life that men may open
for themselves, if courage be the better element of their curi-
osity. One door in Cavender's house would open to justice if
he should give himself up to the law, and admit his guilt. For
he did take Laramie's life; and though there may have been
"reasons"—that is the one fact in his keeping. The opening of
that particular door would also grant him a partial light of
peace. But Laramie is still speaking,

Who spurned your treasure as an angry king
Might throw his crown away, and in his madness
Not know what he had done till all was done.
But who are we to say when all is done?
Was ever an insect flying between two flowers
Told less than we are told of what we are?
Cavender, there may still be hidden for you
A meaning in your house why you are here.[6]

Robinson characterizes Cavender's progress in the valley of
his doubts most subtly when he depicts his terror, not at the
face of truth, but at its source—for it is "the warning told in his
own voice."

Suddenly Cavender is aware that Laramie, as he had expected throughout that she would be, is gone. He waits for
the law to find him in the house of his guilt. The removal of the

---

[5] *Ibid.*, p. 99.   [6] *Ibid.*, pp. 99-100.

lie of his living will give him his freedom from the twists of wonder. Now it matters little that hands stronger than his have made his hands do what they did. He has opened the door to justice—and there is light. But meanwhile he is afraid of its peace, which is suddenly gratuitous. "He has not earned or contemplated it." He does not fear justice or "the laws of men along with older laws and purposes." Cavender begins to understand that the laws of nature tacitly provide a justice which no individual can alter. "This could not be peace that frightened him with wonder," for through the silence of the house it was suddenly "as if Laramie had answered him."

In analyzing this justice, the reader will see that it is not derived from the moralistic sense of justice or providence or punishment and reward. This natural justice is primarily the inevitable consequence of deeds; a theory perhaps reminiscent of Spencer, if not of Dante. It is not to be viewed in the light of reward or punishment; it has no such arbitrary value or meaning. The moral quality of a deed lies in its inevitable consequences. In this poem, at least, Robinson eschews moralistic judgment as an arbitrary interpretation. The man who has murdered is doomed to death by natural law. Civil law, in its wider sense, becomes an adjunct of natural law.

One learns of natural justice through a knowledge of cause and effect. Secondly, interest in natural justice may not find certainty, but it may lead to hope. You examine the hard facts that are, instead of attempting to "anticipate" them by "control," and you get resignation, emancipated from the Christian themes of salvation, forgiveness, and repentance. The doctrine of natural election takes the place of Calvinistic election; since in both systems there is no foreknowledge, there is always room for hope.

The Glory of the Nightingales

The Glory of the Nightingales presents the story of a misunderstanding which became a wedge in the friendship between Malory and Nightingale resulting in jealousy, rivalry, vengeance, and finally mutual remorse.

Trudging alone with his invisible companion, revenge, Malory marks for death Nightingale, who has robbed him of everything important to him. Time, which had once seemed an eternity to Malory, seems now to whip his hours faster as the goal draws nearer. Soon his duty will be done:

> . . . With his work done so righteously,
> Dying would not be much to pay for death,
> Which was attuned and indispensable
> To quivering destiny. No surer part
> Was yet assigned to man for a performance
> Than one that was for Malory, who must act,
> Or leave the stage a failure.[7]

Malory feels that with fate on his side he is destined to kill Nightingale for crashing his house down about him.

> . . . There was no life since then;
> For man, even if divine, is mechanism
> While he is here, and so is not himself
> If much of him be broken. Nightingale
> Had shattered Malory . . .[8]

So doggedly does he believe in the value of his purpose that he is glad to be alive until it is accomplished; this done, he is prepared for death, being

---

[7] Robinson, *The Glory of the Nightingales*, 1930, p. 4.
[8] *Ibid.*, pp. 4–5.

. . . a man of dreams more than of deeds—
Dreams that had not abundantly come true.[9]

Nightingale had always wanted a mansion by the sea, but "he had lost, like many in winning, more than he had won." He had recognized his effect on Malory, but he had rationalized his advantages and aloneness as the result of possessing too much strength to permit choice in the matter. Nightingale firmly believes Malory ungrateful and unwise to meddle with fate. He should have realized that his fate was predestined and that submission to that fate was the only possible course to follow. Having failed to do this, Malory was forgotten and unenvied. The word "unenvied" epitomizes Nightingale's standard of success. He feels that each man has his part to play according to unalterable rules and that he is therefore not responsible for Malory's failure.

Nature, that made the tree, had made the worm,
And Nightingale was not responsible.[10]

Malory recognizes his relative unimportance in the face of an inevitable change rolling onward oblivious of his existence or the needs thereof. Although his neighbors had been estranged since he had destroyed their faith, Malory is assured that his way may have been inscrutable, but right. He and Agatha (now quiet in the city of the dead) would be quiet together when it was all over. Patiently he had endured

The wingless crawl of time in his pursuit
And conquest of invisible destroyers . . .[11]

Malory does not wait for fate. He believes he can take it into his own hands, and be,

[9] Robinson, *The Glory of the Nightingales*, 1930, p. 6.
[10] *Ibid.*, p. 9. [11] *Ibid.*, p. 11.

> . . . as God intended him to be,
> And then forgot. So Malory must be fate,
> Or more than fate, doing God's work, or fate's,
> Or whatsoever the best name of it
> Might be . . . [12]

This self-given usurpation of omnipotence fades as the poem continues, and Malory's defeat through nature's defeat of Nightingale becomes increasingly apparent. Malory was wrong in thinking that he could take Nightingale's life and his own that day; he did neither, and again had no choice in the matter.

And so, sharing his plan with Agatha under the earth, Malory feels that Agatha would somehow be happy to know that his daemonic dream is about to become a present reality. Malory shares the strange old conception of immortality and duty; for him Agatha's ghost cannot be at peace until he and Nightingale have both joined her in whatever world she may now inhabit:

> . . . So he told her all
> He knew—which was abysmally not all
> There was to know. How far he must go back,
> And by what unimaginable guidance,
> To find himself in all his origins
> Was more than science knew—which was as well,
> Also, as other knowledge not for man. [13]

And Agatha, answering his mind's ear, leaves all to silence and to justice after time. Agatha smiles throughout the cemetery scene in which she appears. Is it at Malory's unfounded assurance, or is it that in the clairvoyance granted to the

[12] *Ibid.*, pp. 22–23.   [13] *Ibid.*, pp. 16–17.

departed she knows the end of his journey? Malory resumes his march of vengeance. Arriving at Nightingale's mansion with his hand on the trigger, Malory faces the living dead. In this scene of suspense Robinson, with a master's hand, psychologically juxtaposes the characters, their intentions, and the emphasis of the drama. For Nightingale is a dying man in a wheel chair. "There was no need for killing him; he was dead before his name was called." It is no wonder, then, that "Malory sighed, as one discomfited by destiny too shrewd for chance."

> A tired bacteriologist, seeing him there,
> Might say there was a God. Nature, at least,
> Had never done her work so well before,
> Or saved a man of science so much trouble.[14]

Nightingale's plight, curiously enough, gives Malory a feeling of release, although it leaves him unsatisfied. His new wish is to see God's judgment take its course on Nightingale. And he who had had no fear of dying now has a sick fear of living. Nightingale, on the other hand, suddenly finds a new and momentary hope; for while Malory reflectively stares out to sea, Nightingale confronts him with his drawn revolver. Admitting that either nature or God has beaten him, Malory surrenders. Malory, although his burden has been removed by fate, is possessed by a human fatigue: "he was too tired to care." Malory remains at the mansion and the next morning finds Nightingale recalling that even as a boy, when he was so willing to share everything with Malory, he saw himself as part of a world of traps, lies, conflict, and compromise. Always

> . . . I was the dominant bird,
> Outsinging and outshining and outflying

[14] Robinson, *The Glory of the Nightingales*, 1930, p. 35.

Everything else. . .
I was a man aware that each man carried
Only the lamp the Lord had given to him.
I raised myself no higher than others held me,
And therefore was a brother who understood.
I was a light that would be shining always,
A light for generations to remember.
I was a sort of permanent morning star.
I was the Glory of the Nightingales.[15]

When Agatha had come to Sharon, Nightingale realized that his triumph of all worldly things had been empty without her. And he would have had her, if strange chance had not induced him to introduce Malory to her. Malory stood between him and the door to happiness. Agatha might have, despite her conscience, loved Nightingale through pity, and she would have been subsequently unhappy. Yet Nightingale, with all his power, could not make her love him. If he had shown more understanding of the situation and of his conscience, he would have spared himself much misery; but his vanity would not permit it. He attributes his present pliability, not to his conscience, but to a horrible realization that surrender is necessary, for without Agatha he had nothing. This awakening was at first irritated by surprise and unbelief, later by hate. He was surprised that there was something he could not have and amazed at being capable of such hate. Though it has not been apparent, he has been disturbed by the "surprises of necessity." Attributing all his errors, misfortunes, and hate to the devil of ambition who has been at work within him, he still refuses to blame himself for anything. "There was no way of knowing" what might have happened if he had acted dif-

[15] *Ibid.*, pp. 53-54.

ferently. It was not Nightingale's fault if Malory took his
financial advice and if the investment had a disastrous result.
He admits that in thus wrecking Malory's world, he destroyed
Agatha. He had a fire to destroy Malory; but the fire was the
dark kind that gave no light, and he could not realize what
would happen to Agatha.

Now Malory feels himself without hate and without friends,
but with a new desire for life—with a new desire for rest, for
which he could find no restraint and no explicit reason. While
Nightingale talks, Malory watches the waves and gleans a
message from the waters.

> There were too many of them to be dismissed
> By one whose life was only a little more
> Of time than one of theirs. If theirs were lost,
> Why should not his be lost and be as nothing
> In a more stormy and unsounded ocean
> Than ever filled the valleys of a world
> For men to weigh and measure? [16]

In contrast with Malory, who is sure of nothing save broken
and irrevocable time, his friend, a more positive person, certain
of the vanity of regrets and repentance, is certain, too, of the
value of the coming years. Still unable to say why he acted as
he did (unless he attributes it to devils) and unable to say why
Agatha was an innocent sacrifice, he does know that Malory,
the physician, has a purpose in life—a purpose to be fulfilled
with the mansion as a hospital. This would give Malory the
lonely joy of being of service to society, of not being wasted,
because of his attempt to find light for others. Nightingale, by
this act of charity, feels relieved of his former burdens and
moralizes that one should live so as not to be alone.

[16] Robinson, *The Glory of the Nightingales*, 1930, p. 73.

While Malory is on an errand concerning the new project, Nightingale commits suicide. Perhaps Nightingale's dark way of life was necessary.

> . . . There is, meanwhile,
> A native light for others, but none born
> Of penitence, or of man's fear to die.
> Fear is not light, and you were never afraid.
> You were blind, Nightingale, but never afraid;
> And even when you were blind, you may have seen,
> Darkly, where you were going, and where you are.
> For where you are tonight, there was your place;
> And your dark glass is broken.[17]

Now that Nightingale is dead, Malory is left with a new life of struggle in the darkness, "guided by a light that would be his and Nightingale's."

It is only in the light of the poem's conclusion that the personalities or points of view of the characters take on new and added significance. Thus we see that Malory changes completely; his former desire to die after murdering Nightingale is supplanted by a desire to live and help bear the burden of humanity—to live and to follow his light. He is always possessed by fear, though the object of the fear varies; first it is fear of death, then of life. The moment of transition occurs when Malory, liberated from duty as he sees it, attains a new point of view toward duty. Similarly, when Nightingale has explained himself to Malory and has relinquished his mansion and his wealth, he finds a kind of release in duty. Nightingale has not grown as much as Malory. To the very end of his life his pleasure consists in maneuvering power over others. The noble element enters in his sanguine redirection of this

[17] *Ibid.*, p. 82.

power. For this new ambition in Malory is an element of the power Nightingale possessed.

Faith in man, in oneself, and "all there's left to die for" becomes all there's left to live for, so that Malory becomes resigned to life rather than to death. He had lost his faith when he was wronged by Nightingale; but ironically it is Nightingale who gives him a new kind of faith or purpose in living. Despite the liberation, there is no real freedom or opportunity to rest. Instead of being driven to vengeance, Malory is now driven to aid others. It is simply a change of direction with no real peace for Malory. It is a shifting of burdens from the destructive to the creative; from revenge to devotion; from death to life. It is the same intensity of activity and of conscience, but with greater achievement, with a new light for guidance.

Matthias at the Door

This poem is a profound analysis of the tragedy of love, and one of Robinson's favorite expositions of his philosophy. Matthias had saved the life of Timberlake, his best friend. As a result the latter has never told Natalie, whom Matthias married, of his love for her. Years later Timberlake, before committing suicide, admits his love to Natalie, who expresses her reciprocal passion. Although Matthias, having learned of the situation, begins to distrust his wife, he decides that it would be of mutual benefit for him to pretend that nothing has ever happened to disturb the happiness of either. The poem presents two extremes of complacency—the younger self-satisfied Matthias, who has wealth, position, and a wife whom he loves and who seems to be as sincere as he is, and the older, wiser Matthias, who becomes resigned to life when he attempts to face its truth. The manifest poles of his development are his comfortable complacency at the outset and his resignation at the poem's conclusion. The theme of the poem in its barest statement is that resignation is the fruit of knowledge.

Having become aware of his wife's true feelings, Matthias has two courses of action. He chooses reconciliation in preference to complaint, which implies failure in a life otherwise buoyant with honor. We see the relation between honor and failure in Natalie's thoughts of

> . . . Garth, who in time gone
> Had sat there with them and as carelessly
> Promised himself the wealth that was for him
> His pillow and his dream—not that he cared
> For wealth, but for the quieting of some tongues.
> Matthias, long familiar with it all,
> Had been for years indulgent and amused,
> But now for years had nodded, and sometimes
> Had yawned. It was his tongue, more than another,
> Garth would have quieted. Now Garth was quiet,
> Natalie thought, and missed him. She had liked him—
> Partly for his futility, perhaps,
> Having one something like it as her own
> To nourish and conceal.[18]

Robinson makes the point that while it deserves no bright honor, there is nothing dishonorable about failure.

> "Matthias means
> 'Unfortunate,' maybe," said Timberlake.
> "Our words have our complexions, like our skins.
> Accomplishment and honor are not the same,

[18] Robinson, *Matthias at the Door*, 1931, p. 32.

[111]

Matthias; and one may live without the other."
"Yes, Timberlake. A man may throw himself
Utterly to the dogs and say to them
That his accomplishment is less than honor.
The dogs would be impressed." Matthias chuckled.

"Of course," Natalie said. "He should say, 'Dogs,
I am not much, but I am honorable.
So wag your tails at me, and do not bark.'
That would soon quiet them." [19]

He first identifies dishonor with failure; then denies both. His answer to the question "what is honor?" is that success and honor do not go together and that honor is a foolish aim, as is shown by his whimsical reference to the dogs. For Robinson honesty has nothing to do with the honorable. By putting himself in the suicide's place the poet makes a pretence of not judging. In such a situation, no one admits judgment. Speaking of the suicide of Garth, Timberlake answers Natalie's question, "how do you know where Garth has gone," with "I don't."

Analyzing the love of Natalie and Timberlake, Robinson sees no freedom in love, for "satisfaction" does not solve the problem. They might have been married,

. . . and one day I might have killed you,
And then myself. That would have been all right.
We should have killed each other, and so known
That we had lived a little before we died.
Can you see there no comfort? What do you see
In this? It looks to me a waste of being,

[19] Robinson, *Matthias at the Door*, 1931, pp. 24–25.

And a more desolate foolishness for knowing
Just what it is.[20]

Natalie sees them as three fools consciously destroying the houses they built for themselves—these houses representing dreams of happiness. The dreams of Natalie and Timberlake are ruins, but Matthias, believing that his wife loved him, has built his house "happily on a lie." Even as success has nothing to do with honor, so with intelligence. Matthias's original poise results, not from honor and success, but from a dearth of the truth that the others possess. Timberlake believes that Matthias would be different if he saw differently—that is, if he "learned some things that many a man must never know."

> . . . "I'm afraid,"
> He said, "that he may soon learn some of them.
> Garth, I've a notion, tore a few farewell holes
> In the rich web of his complacency,
> Letting some truth come in. Whether Matthias
> Would see the truth, or would see only holes,
> Is a new question. I'm not answering that . . ."[21]

Timberlake had not shown Matthias the truth, because the latter had once saved his life. Timberlake has paid his debt of friendship with a frustrate love that resulted in and was his suicide. For him life was a bewildering kaleidoscope.

> There's a malignance in the distribution
> Of our effects and faculties. It is nature,
> And our faith makes it more. If it's no more,
> Garth waited longer than was logical
> For a good atheist who believed himself

[20] *Ibid.*, p. 38.   [21] *Ibid.*, p. 39.

And life a riot of cells and chemistry—
If he believed it. You say you believe it,
But in that curious woman's apprehension
Of yours there broods a doubt that frightens you
More than annihilation.[22]

Robinson believes a thoroughgoing skeptic would not wish to live at all. Garth had waited until life became unbearable—showing that he had had hope. Garth and Natalie, being atheists, should not have been afraid to die, yet she had a fear of death and clung to a faith, while Garth's fear was of complacency. Timberlake is not sure that what he did was "the best way out," because he fears that if he had disturbed Matthias's "complacent faith" in Natalie, the fire that would "leave a mask on friendship would be a brand on love." If they had told Matthias the truth, matters might have been worse.

                    . . . and time,
Developing combustion, might have achieved
An earthquake, or a woman-quake, within you
That would have blown our problematic house
To chips and flinders, and ourselves as well;
Which would have been more picturesque than pleasant,
More ruinous than unique. The same has happened;
And I have helped, and burned my fingers helping,
To rescue out of hot and smoking ruins
A few things yet worth saving. It's dark work,
And mostly smoke and ashes. Half the grief
Of living is our not seeing what's not to be
Before we see too well. You have Matthias,
And a safe nest. I'm ready enough to know
How far that is from nothing.[23]

[22] Robinson, *Matthias at the Door,* 1931, p. 41.   [23] *Ibid.,* pp. 42–43.

This reference to man's not seeing until he sees too well is another form of Robinson's lament that one's light is a revelation rather than a guide. This quotation is also important as an analysis of love and passion. Timberlake seems to think Natalie's love was short-lived passion, a temporary flame which having flared once would have left them in darkness again. Perhaps he would have provided for her as Matthias did. He reasons here that her material comfort had been more important than a short romance which might leave her with nothing "left to do but laugh—unless she cries." This is another example of Robinson's laughter at human folly—laughter which is a favorable alternative to self-pity at the sight of tragedy.

When Matthias finally discovers that Natalie does not love him, he decides that it is better to keep their ship sailing, for "to sink would be conspicuous and dramatic." Natalie shows her appreciation.

> . . . "If I could find
> Your God, or what you call it, to believe in,
> Matthias, I could praise him for creating
> A world no worse than this. He might have done it,
> If he had tried, and how much worse a mess
> We mortals might be making of ourselves
> Is only for him to say." . . . "If my faith went out,"
> He said, "my days to be would all be night—
> A night without a dawn, and with no lamp.
> You should know that. God knows you should know that." [24]

Here again the truth is of small consequence, although it has the power to shatter his complacency and his life. As Matthias sees the situation,

[24] *Ibid.*, p. 51.

[115]

. . . The trouble with you,
And me, and a few millions who are like us,
Is that we live so long to know so little,
And are not willing then to know ourselves.
Where are the mysteries in us that require
So much dramatic fuss? [25]

Matthias is not Robinson. The former cannot see why there should be so much fuss, whereas Robinson would say nothing else is worth the fuss but this knowledge of the mysteries in us.

During the poem's closing movement pride displaces Matthias's former gratefulness. Knowledge makes him proud. This fundamental theme indicates a consequence of revelation. Truth has no practical value, for it does not settle daily problems. It removes fear, permitting one to face his faith with seeing eyes. Robinson's psychology of fear is not that people fear ignorance and doubt, but that they fear belief. Self-satisfaction lasts until they see the light; or at least they enjoy relative happiness. Light throws a silhouette of doubt around their beliefs. Matthias has never doubted or feared that Natalie loved him. He has not known the fear of ignorance or of doubt; but when he learns the truth, his faith in former beliefs is shattered, and he knows the fear that upsets his complacency. However, he still demands a modicum of ostensible success; even without complacency he can still insist "on keeping their ship sailing."

The basic study does not center in Garth, who was simple; it is the transformation of Matthias's character when he receives the sacrament of the light. Garth does not see the light and does not want to see it; not giving the matter much

[25] Robinson, *Matthias at the Door*, 1931, p. 61.

thought, he simply commits suicide. But the effect of the light on the other three is important, for the light has made each considerate of the other two to the exclusion of himself, each showing a sacrificing loyalty to the others.

> . . . Time was a traitor to Matthias,
> Who had believed in time and trusted it
> Without a fear of its betraying him,
> As faith will trust a grave without a promise;
> And in their way Matthias and his pride
> Were traitors—if an insurrection sleeps
> While its indignities and inspirations
> Are moving and awakening in the dark.[26]

Robinson presents light as essentially timeless, therefore, lifeless and faithless; for life exists in the darkness of time. Light cannot of itself destroy the force of passion; but, as in the case of Timberlake's love for Natalie, it can transform the tragic consequences of passion into the peaceful understanding of tragedy. Thus as Garth, Timberlake, and Natalie see the light, each commits suicide, but death has different qualities for each of them. Garth knows intense joy, followed by intense sorrow; the others know resignation as well. The principle of life consists of activity and passion, not of knowledge. Knowledge is a cold light, bringing the weak to the door of death and a darkness which is beyond the revealing lance of inner, personal light, or truth.

Talifer

Talifer is a Robinsonian comedy of love in which conventional frustration results from a poorly-matched marriage. Instead of marrying Althea, who loves him, Talifer marries

[26] *Ibid.*, p. 54.

Karen, a cold, intellectual woman who hardly loves and even fears him. Dr. Quick, friend of the three, having unsuccessfully tried to win both women, eventually resigns himself to his social failure. The kind of peace he sees is treated as something essentially trivial and comic. The comedy reveals the scientific attitude as typified by Dr. Quick, to whom life is biologically simple. While the other characters have found life a tragedy, he does not find fate necessarily tragic. Dr. Quick believes that destiny sometimes works for happiness, even if the joy is for others and even if his own contentment is not the kind he would have preferred. In this poem, whose tone is essentially comic, Robinson draws a peace that is ironical and superficial. From this ironic treatment we gather that *Talifer* was probably intended to be sharply humorous rather than profoundly philosophical. One illustration of Robinson's descriptive whimsy is his portrait of young Samuel, Talifer's child, in his "chariot." The baby is a "new person who sees more than he thinks he'd better say."

> The son and heir,
> From his perambulator, scanned his father
> Somewhat as if in doubt of his importance;
> And having striven in vain to change his mind,
> He fixed a beaming gaze upon his mother,
> And with a language of one syllable
> And of two hands, made himself understood.
> She lifted him from his imprisonment
> And held him as if he were naturally
> A part of her, and was no trouble to hold—
> Which was a mystery still to Talifer,
> Who found him fearsome and irregular,
> And of no constant length or magnitude.

Like one who had read somewhere in a treatise
How it was done, he touched his infant's nose
With an abrupt unfaltering forefinger,
And sat back with an air of one who knew
What was expected and could always do it—
All with a shrewd smile of encouragement
And confidence between him and his son,
Who promptly welcomed and rewarded it
With a malignant scowl.[27]

　　　. . . Young Samuel,
Too long misused, employed his power of sound
As an elected and clairvoyant martyr
Might publish the injustice of his birth,
With none to notice him.[28]

Even Quick's scientific determinism is not tragic as when he speaks to Althea.

　　　　　"You are not
Indifferent; you are desperate," said he;
"And that's not good for ladies living alone." [29]

The conversation between Talifer and Quick illustrates the latter's problems. His opinion of himself has been influenced by his uncle, yet he understands himself and gives a sardonic "peace" to his "honorable" frustration:

Before he died, my sinful uncle said
That I should never attain. I was like Reuben,
He said, because like him I was unstable,
And told me where to find him in the Bible.
He died, leaving all to me—and to my honor.
He must have enjoyed that. And since he died,

27 Robinson, *Talifer*, 1933, p. 87.　　28 *Ibid.*, p. 97.　　29 *Ibid.*, p. 37.

Honor has only made me miserable,
And worn to weary grief my fiery spirit;
Honor has been the cross that I have carried,
Unseen and unrewarded, all these years.
Don't wish that you might have it.[30]

     . . . he sighed,
With an untroubled comfortable envy
Of mightier men than he, who had performed
Or thought immortally, and had left their deeds
And thoughts behind them for mankind to cherish.
He sighed again, fearing that he would leave
Only what undiscriminating fortune
Had left to him; and if his pride was quiet
Because of that, his grief to be unwritten
Among the mighty was an easier pang
To bear than endless pain and destitution—
Of which in lives around him he had seen
Far more than was a pleasure. On the whole,
He fancied he was not the most accurst
Of men . . .[31]

 Despite all the comfortable chords of resigned humor, there
is a serious, almost tragic, note sounded in Dr. Quick's speech
to young Samuel. He briefly, but analytically, sums up the
difficulties of the Talifer romance, which are the result of
ignorance and impatience. Man's suspicion or wrong in-
ferences, in place of knowledge, makes "man pay variously,
with more than coin of earth, for more than his terrestrial ap-
paratus." Ignorance, however, should not be reason for undue
suffering or suicide, according to Quick's scientific point of

[30] Robinson, *Talifer*, 1933, p. 20.   [31] *Ibid.*, p. 70.

view. He does not understand why Althea should have paid so great a price to teach her husband that his happiness could come from her rather than from Karen; but as long as it made her happy to do so, it must have been worth it. All men are "omniscient" as babies, but apparently they grow more foolish with age. He sees Talifer's doom (that is, his former doom, or tragedy, with Karen) as the result of his "having all God may give" yet clamoring for the "unpossessed." Quick had also suffered when his friend in a search for peace made his first unhappy marriage with Karen; however, now that Talifer and Althea are married the doctor is untroubled, for he considers it the results of destiny that she should give Talifer "more than he deserved" and that he, Quick, received none of the love he desired and deserved. After his infatuation with the "Fish-Venus," the passionless but beautiful Karen, Talifer "came to daylight and saw truth," or Althea.

Dr. Quick seems to accept his life as something predestined, whereas Talifer exhibits greater powers of self-assertion. Quick stresses his own importance in his ability to step between Karen and her husband in order to bring about Talifer's second marriage. There seems to be the distinction that while one can help others with their problems—a service which may be a part of destiny—one cannot do much to gain one's own happiness. If he had not interposed, the situation might have been entirely different; but only temporarily so, for eventually fate must win to its ends.

> . . . Time and Events,
> Your father's team of galloping tortoises,
> Who arrived suddenly one afternoon,
> Would have come sometime anyhow; and your mother,
> Not fitted for the part of an impatient

Griselda, would have frowned unfeelingly
On numerous men of merit, like myself,
And still would have been waiting for your father,
Who is not nearly so remarkable,
Or so celestially worth waiting for,
As she believes he is. But fate said yes,
And so it was. And so good Doctor Quick,
As always, did the work and had no pay.[32]

[32] Robinson, *Talifer*, 1933, pp. 93–94.

Dragons and Chimneys

Dionysus in Doubt

DIONYSUS IN DOUBT reveals, probably more than any other single poem, Robinson's ideas on social philosophy. The apparent reasonableness and truth in the poem are to be recognized through the initially deceptive veil of a kind of high inebriation. The intensely metrical dithyramb mounts steadily from a somewhat sober criticism of American civilization to a crescendo of indignation. It is perhaps the poet's tactful intention to have the expression of radical ideas treated under the guise of intoxication. However that may be, the theme of radical individualism, with an emphasis on freedom as opposed to uniformity, is elucidated. The theme is not a new one in the schools of philosophy, but here it is treated freshly and cleverly. To have the wine god voice his sentiments on the whirling globe, is, to say the least, unique. As sobriety fades out, doubt enters to take its place. A great deal of the "conversation" is realized as tense emotion rather than calculated utterance resulting from cool reflection.

The social situation is regarded, and its good and evil features are enumerated. The laws of the nation are too numerous and meaningless—"arbitrary ways of capturing and harnessing salvation." Yet in spite of the abundance of unnecessary legislation, "predatory love in freedom's name" flourishes. Freedom misdirected becomes a thing to fear rather than to desire. What most men consider freedom is a beguiling convention that really limits self-expression. Such a brand of freedom breeds restraint. It creates a vicious circle, ostensibly enlarging to permit more liberty, but in fact absorbing and circumscribing the decreasing rights of the individual. The irony of the situation is revealed in man's attempts at legislation to limit the effects of nature, which to Robinson is the underlying cause of limitations. "Herd-servitude" would moronize the million for the few. Nature is concerned more with benefits for the million than for the few. Still, if the few were not encouraged to be original, progress would be retarded.

> Oblivious of the many-venomed ways
> Attendant on their failing who should fail,
> By soporific tyranny misled
> Into a specious maze
> Where vermin unsupposable are bred,
> You may not see a sign of the snake's tail
> Whereon you are to tread.[1]

This quotation is very similar to the philosophy of government expressed in *King Jasper*. Rulers, misguided by ambition, selfishness, and "predatory love," show no consideration for the millions and are oblivious to the undercurrents of revolt resulting from the evils of poor ruling. Even the metaphor of the snake parallels in kind, if not degree, the dragon of *King Jasper*. At times democracy may be as tyrannical in its methods against individual freedom as is monarchy. This form of democracy is still in its early stages of development. Hence its evils are not as conspicuous as they will be when age has hardened the blood lines of change.

[1] Robinson, *Dionysus in Doubt*, 1925, p. 20.

> In weakness indirectly there was hope
> For an unransomed kidnapped juvenile
> Miscalled Democracy.[2]

Nevertheless there is hope for the situation. Latent intelligence, which is "so long in coming," will burgeon in its time. But the weeds of "hypocrisy, timidity, and sloth" already flourish and choke the soil against the coming of salvation. One finds man

> . . . almost everywhere
> Perniciously at prayer
> For consummation and a furtherance
> Of his benevolent ingrained repression
> Of the next man's possession.

> . . .

> Sometimes it may be better not to know
> Than to be stoned for knowing.

> . . .

> "All that is coming will come soon enough,"
> He said, "and it will be no balm for pride;
> And one forlorn prediction will achieve
> No remedy or reprieve.
> There are some fiery letters never learned
> Till children who are reading them are burned
> Before they are aware of any fire.
> Remember that, all you that would aspire,
> Unsinged and all alone,
> To the unseen and the discredited,
> And to the best for you unknown." [3]

[2] *Ibid.*   [3] *Ibid.*, pp. 21–22.

There are other evils: selfishness, fraud, dissension, danger, distrust. These self-defined vices make for the negation of expression in the individual and in the state. Looking less cursorily over the land reveals too many sleepers, people subdued by "defeat, indifference, and forsworn command." Too many are lax and amiable still in the face of error and insincerity. And there are always those whose shortsightedness is worse than blindness.

> Too many are recommended not to see,
> Or loudly to suggest,
> That opulence, compromise, and lethargy
> Together are not the bravest or the best
> Among the imaginable remedies
> For a young world's unrest;
> Too many are not at all distressed
> Or noticeably ill at ease
> With nature's inner counsel when it means
> That if a drowsy wisdom blinks and leans
> Too much on legioned innocence
> Armed only with a large mistake,
> Something is due to shake . . . [4]

This summation of evils finds fuller expansion in *King Jasper*, although they are not treated in a dramatic form. The line "something is due to shake" finds its equivalent in the symbol of the falling chimneys in Jasper's land. In both poems there are too many who have "learned expediently how not to think." The tirade against convention and uniformity is subtly humorous and full of vigor.

[4] Robinson, *Dionysus in Doubt*, 1925, p. 25.

Sometimes I wonder what machine
Your innocence will employ . . .
When all are niched and ticketed and all
Are standardized and unexceptional,
To perpetrate complacency and joy
Of uniform size and strength;
Sometimes I ponder whether you have seen,
Or contemplated over much down there,
The treacherous way that you are now pursuing,
Or by just what immeasurable expense
Of unexplained omnipotence
You are to make it lead you anywhere
Than to the wonder of a sick despair
That waits upon a gullible undoing.[5]

This system shows a complete disregard for the individualism so vital to Robinson. Although men may not want to heed the truth, eventually and "unwillingly they must." They will no longer "praise the obvious for the absolute" or think that they can direct destiny. The following lines of Dionysus are similar to the words of Amaranth who cannot explain why he must act as he does except that God wills it so:

The gods have methods that are various,
Not always to themselves too clear;
And mine that may destroy you or defend you
Are gentle to those of Him that you revere
So blindly while they rend you,
Till mercifully and at last they end you—
If so they do.[6]

[5] *Ibid.*, pp. 26–27.   [6] *Ibid.*, pp. 29–30.

Dionysus warns man to reorganize the state so that even a blind individual may regain his identity, despite the bitterness against bad laws that are "like bad pilots authorized to see not and to care not where they steer." There is a note of optimism in the intimation that

> Some would have more things done
> Today than are begun—
> Things that will yet, in spite of the existence
> Of an unformed and misapplied assistance,
> Come properly to pass . . .[7]

It has been the contention of the superficial critics, or rather would-be critics of Robinson, that he has not faced the pertinent problems of his day. They have examined his poetry for contemporary industrial scenery and problematics. Not finding these, they have pontifically pronounced judgment. *Dionysus in Doubt* does not treat, it is true, peculiarly current problems; it does treat the political principles and problems which confront any thinking individual and reveals the fact that Robinson was not indifferent to the social issues of his time.

King Jasper

"The idea for 'King Jasper' had come to Robinson, walking down State Street in Boston during the bank holiday, following the inauguration of Franklin Roosevelt, and the name of his protagonist was that of the mine down which the last of his patrimony had vanished thirty-five years before. He was distrustful of a contemporaneous theme but could not resist the temptation to write what he called his 'treatise on economics.' He gave the poem a triple significance—first, as a story of six unhappy beings, caught in a cataclysm of all that is

[7] Robinson, *Dionysus in Doubt*, 1925, pp. 30–31.

life to them; then, as a symbolic drama of the disintegration of the capitalistic system; and, last, as an allegory of ignorance and knowledge and aspiration." [8]

With the Kantian imperative "do your duty" as a problem, *King Jasper* becomes a study of character growth and moral development varying according to the extent and direction of the individual's sense of responsibility and value. For possessing a conscience or for lack of one each character becomes a case in point. Conscience appears most obviously in "bad conscience"—in those vague restraints whose pressure is felt, although their purpose is not seen. This type of conscience appears in Queen Honoria.

> . . . Honoria
> Might have been happier had she never felt
> The touch of hidden fingers everywhere,
> On everything, and sometimes all but seen them. [9]
> . . . Or, were those hands
> That she felt everywhere on everything
> Blasting already with unseen decay
> Walls, roofs, and furniture, and all there was
> For her to feel and see and never to know.
> She watched the flame and wondered why it was
> That she was always waiting, and for what. [10]

To Honoria, Jasper is king in the fullest sense of the title.

> Your chimneys are the landmark of your power.
> Without them, I know best what I should be. [11]

King Jasper's conscience, on the other hand, does not haunt him, nor are there hidden fingers everywhere, for him.

[8] Hagedorn, *Edwin Arlington Robinson*, p. 369.
[9] Robinson, *King Jasper*, 1935, p. 2.   [10] *Ibid.*   [11] *Ibid.*, p. 5.

> I'm wishing that your eyes were finding more
> For mine to share with them, and less that's hidden.[12]

The king believes it is Prince Jasper who troubles her and asks, "What are we going to make of him?" The queen's reply is the keynote to the poem as a study in the bondage of one generation to another.

> What shall we make of him, you ask? I ask,
> What shall he make of us? If you are strong,
> And the world says you are, he may be stronger,
> And with a wilder strength. He is still young,
> And so must have his visions. If you fear
> He sees today too far beyond your chimneys,
> Why be alarmed? Be quiet, and let him grow.
> The chimneys are still there.[13]

Jasper laments that the prince's filial pride in these chimneys is in, not what others call supremacy, but an abstraction he calls a dragon. Throughout the poem the chimneys, symbolic of the material products of ambition, harbor the dragons of corruption and deceit. The king continues with a description of Zoë, his new daughter-in-law.

> Meanwhile his occupation is a woman
> He calls his wife. She is too free and holy,
> Or so he says, to let herself be bound
> Or tangled in the flimsy nets or threads
> Of church or state.
>
> .   .   .
>
> equipped
> To sting the mightiest spiders of convention
> And fly away from them as free as ever.[14]

[12] Robinson, *King Jasper*, 1935, p. 2.   [13] *Ibid.*, p. 6.   [14] *Ibid.*, pp. 6–7.

The last two lines epitomize Zoë's part in the poem. She has come, a free spirit, to linger in the bondage of the palace long enough to have a disastrous but enlightening effect on each of the characters and then proceeds on her way in life, alone. King Jasper warns the queen.

> For better or worse, you may as well accept her;
> For I'm afraid you must, or lose your son.[15]

The prince does not trouble the queen. Her meaningful answer is

> I know them; and I know whose hands they are,
> Jasper; and I have known for a long time.[16]

For the king these hands are living and invincible. For the queen they belong to a ghost with power to crush.

The prince introduces Zoë, who expresses the younger generation's attempt to change the morals of their elders. The queen is totally unsympathetic to Zoë and the transition she represents, and she interprets her arrival as the end of the queen's world.

> . . . If this means the end
> Of my world, and if I have lost my way
> In a new wilderness, with no road back
> To where I was, I'd rather be there alone,
> And die there, than go on.[17]

The queen's intolerance of Zoë and the manners of a new era mark the beginning of the tragic end awaiting her.

> And quietly, with a pallor-covered rage
> Half-blinding her, she walked out like a queen.[18]

The king is aware that Zoë is laughing at him and wonders at this laughter. In her characteristic, uncanny manner, she

[15] *Ibid.*, p. 7.   [16] *Ibid.*, p. 12.   [17] *Ibid.*, p. 15.   [18] *Ibid.*, p. 16.

has read his premonitions of destructive hands at work in his kingdom.

> The mightiest are the blindest; and I wonder
> Why they forget themselves in histories
> They cannot read because they have no sight.
> What useless chronicles of bloody dust
> Their deeds will be sometime! And all because
> They cannot see behind them or before them,
> And cannot see themselves. For them there must
> Be multitudes of cold and unseen hands
> That reach for them and touch them horribly
> When they're alone.[19]

The prince now introduces a new danger. He informs King Jasper that he saw young Hebron among the chimneys

> Measuring them with a sardonic eye
> As if they were not yours.[20]

Why doesn't the king hang a picture of old Hebron where he can see him, as he once intended? Sarcastically, young Jasper insinuates that his father owes Hebron that and perhaps more.

> "My son, when you are older," said the king,
> Smiling a scowl away, "you will have learned
> That all who have climbed higher than the rest
> Owe the dead more than pictures. If the dead,
> And the long-dead before them, should return
> With ledgers telling us where our debts are cast,
> We should know more than fate sees necessary.
> If Hebron was my friend, I was his friend.
> He died, I lived. And there was no crime there—
> Unless you say there's crime in being alive." [21]

[19] Robinson, *King Jasper*, 1935, pp. 20-21.   [20] *Ibid.*, p. 23.   [21] *Ibid.*

Thus King Jasper rationalizes his debt to Hebron.

The knowledge that Zoë has read his thoughts increasingly disturbs King Jasper, so that he is afraid of being alone. Here we have signs of her effect on his conscience. This inability to be alone and to do things alone is one of Robinson's favorite themes. Jasper's crown troubles him.

> For well he knew, and latterly too well,
> That age, as it came on, was giving him eyes
> To see more surely the dark way behind him
> That he had climbed, with opportunity
> And enterprise to drive him, and to mock him
> Whenever he looked back.[22]

However, it is more than opportunity and enterprise that troubles him. It is a new laughing voice, a voice that might be as warning, scorning, or triumphant as death.

> With sleep no longer even a theme of hope
> To save him as a doom-defying refuge,
> He counted those lost hours until he saw them
> Like dead friends he had slain; and then he slept.[23]

And dreams: Jasper, dead, is alone, climbing rocks, mounting to an ever-receding summit. Some unknown command keeps him from stopping, though he is exhausted and freighted with despair. Finally he meets the once kindly Hebron, whose welcoming voice has notes of scorn and accusation. Has death changed him, or has the king's fear wrought the change? The king no longer feels himself an invincible ruler. The two climb together, Hebron accusing Jasper of hate, deceit, and greed,—while Jasper, attributing his wickedness to fear, admits that it was for power, not for gold, that he so selfishly neglected He-

[22] *Ibid.*, p. 28.   [23] *Ibid.*, p. 29.

bron. His demon has been blind ambition. Hebron forgives Jasper, although the latter's monstrosities have reft him of manhood.

> When I was gone, men said you were a king;
> But you were more. You were almost a kingdom;
> And you forgot that kingdoms are not men.
> They are composite and obscure creations
> Of men, and in a manner are comparable
> To moving and unmanageable machines,
> And somehow are infernally animated
> With a self-interest so omnivorous
> That ultimately they must eat themselves.
> You cannot eat yourself very long and live,
> Jasper . . .[24]

Old Hebron, tired, insists that the king carry him. Jasper now has to endure and stagger under Hebron's weight. He cannot fall and continues with the crushing burden of malice. Did Jasper suppose that he could have all for nothing? It is now his turn to help Hebron in his climb over the rocks. The king hopes that he may fall and die, but he has to climb on and on, always. Begging mercy, he concedes that Hebron stood between him and his fate which made him king. Meanwhile Hebron's weight has increased to the weight of gold that Jasper had stolen. When the latter whines, Hebron maliciously reminds the blind king that his burden is only Hebron's weight. They come to a chasm, narrow enough to attempt and wide enough to swallow them. On the other side stand Zoë and Prince Jasper laughing at the kingly beast of burden. Hebron perceives Jasper's remorse.

[24] Robinson, *King Jasper*, 1935, pp. 35–36.

> . . . With me to carry,
> You know the burden of your worth, and feel it,
> As it accumulates with every step
> An overpowering slow solidity
> That clings, and cripples you the while it grows.
> You said I might have crippled you, and I will.[25]

Jasper imagines he sees Zoë's message as one of salvation and wants to jump, but cannot. His son seems to have lost his respect for him at his hesitancy to shake off "the living load of death that was his philosophy and his life." Zoë promises that if the king has the courage to leap he will throw off the crushing monster and will see his kingdom, his power, his glory as it is and is to be. Hebron recommends that Jasper have faith and jump. It is toward this moment's test that the awful weight has been burdening him. Zoë names his ambition folly—a folly which has blinded him. He has buried his being in a personal desert of golden sand. A symbol of individual enlightenment and freedom, she so charms the king that he, without the will to choose or power to remain, hopefully plunges to a startled safety, as the burden of Hebron vanishes. Zoë cautions the king against desiring her beauty, which is the product of his evil and ignorance. Withal the king has not yet learned restraint; she stabs him, laughing, "poor king! poor fool!"—as he falls into the abyss of darkness. Suddenly the dream ends. At this moment young Hebron arrives, joyfully smiling. He has come for the payment of Jasper's debt to his father. He believes he has found the panacea for an ailing world.

Although young Hebron arouses the reader's sense of justice, his possessive manner evokes no sympathy. Young Hebron

[25] *Ibid.*, p. 43.

fancies an ill fate has destined his father for disaster. Here again, as in the king's dream leap, we are made to feel that the individual has no choice—that circumstances determine action. Hebron remarks that the palace might have been his, but now his house will be the world, which he cannot own and therefore cannot lose. Jasper ridicules this attitude as puerile vision to be displaced by mature wisdom. There is a suggestion, subtly made, that the palace might some day be Hebron's. For Hebron "came, and saw—like Caesar." Zoë, on some pretext or other, comes into the room. Her beauty has its usual effect upon the intruder, but she is vexed by his admiration. Ominously he departs.

> *Auf wiedersehen* . . .
> I'm sorry that my sorrow leaves with you,
> And with the king, a portrait so remote,
> So false and clouded and intangible.[26]

The queen scornfully expresses her hate; the king his tolerance, by explaining Hebron's grievance as a mission or religion.

> . . . For where's the use
> Of Christ dying on a cross, and you being told
> To love your enemies, if you'll only hate them
> Harder, and worse and worse? . . . No, I don't hate him.[27]

Jasper asks Zoë whether her wisdom is man's doom or his savior. She might be a redeemer, but in that case she must keep her freedom. King Jasper regrets that she is too wise to be happy in the world men have made. Zoë maintains that wicked reformers will make the world even worse.

> . . . And wrong prophets, like this Hebron,
> Will sing of blood while others bleed for them.

[26] Robinson, *King Jasper*, 1935, p. 64.   [27] *Ibid.*, p. 66.

They cannot know. Only a few may know;
And they, the wise one said, must go alone.[28]

In analyzing the knife wound, in the dream, she holds it was
not she whom the king feared. It was time and consequences.
Zoë, however, does not fear time. When the chimneys crumble,
where will his kingdom be? The king, especially, should not
dread knives or time, for he has used both carelessly as imple-
ments. Similarly, he should know better than to ask why the
chimneys are doomed.

The king needs no more dreams to understand that fate was
destroying his chimneys.

There were no kings of earth mighty enough
To make them rest. There would be kings always,
Crowned or uncrowned, or all would be alike—
A thought so monstrous that King Jasper shivered
As long as it was in him.[29]

Prince Jasper, foreseeing the return of Hebron, suggests that
his parents go away. The king insists that he shall remain but
is equally firm that Honoria think of her own well-being and
leave the castle.

The prince alone is without a trace of sorrow, and he asks his
father what he thinks of God and His work. He and Zoë imagine that for kings the devil is God. The dragon in the chimney
is the product of his omnipotence. The prince is about to in-
quire after his mother, when his father enters to tell him that
she is dead.

. . . Your mother, her life long,
Said sorrow had no other friend than silence.
It was her way—and may have been the best.[30]

[28] *Ibid.*, p. 70.   [29] *Ibid.*, p. 73.   [30] *Ibid.*, p. 89.

King Jasper is waiting for his reward—freedom which he hoped would be a darkness without dreams. Zoë tries to convince him that God's purpose includes the failings of royalty. She further attempts to appease him by saying that even ambitious kings, without consciences, have contributed toward progress. For the prince the conflict resolves itself into two possible courses of action: he can help the king or desert him. Zoë believes it is his duty to remain with his father, but she must go on her way alone, for she is life. She cannot die. Unlike his disturbed son, King Jasper is beginning to feel more at ease. As he looks through the gloom spread over his chimneys and kingdom, he sees

> A shining and a rising of wild light
> That never was there before.[31]
>
> . . .
>
> . . . One light followed
> Another, wherever the planted spawn of doom
> Bloomed into flame and rose to find the sky
> And burn the firmament. He had forgotten
> Zoë, and all that she had said of death.
> Here was a death worth dying; here was a pyre
> Of life worth dying for.[32]

The chimneys fall. The king's joy in living and having his kingdom is followed by an intense fear at seeing it ruined by the light. Such an end is inevitable. The prince feels there is no way out for them. Perhaps his mother's solution was the best. Another chimney collapses. Admitting that Zoë knows his son better than he does, the king dies. Just then a loud shot with a "noise that might have been the crash of judgment on a

---

[31] Robinson, *King Jasper*, 1935, p. 97.   [32] *Ibid.*, p. 98.

dishonored world" rings out—the prince is murdered. Young
Hebron enters—a lustful criminal, frenzied with avenging hate
and Zoë's enigmatic beauty. She greets him with scorn and a
despairing pity.

> . . . let your poor, sick, stricken soul
> Suffer until it feels; and let it feel
> Until it sees. You will have died meanwhile,
> But who knows death? [33]

Hebron wants Zoë to remain with him. He must have her
gleams of knowledge.

> You do not know that you and I together
> Are God's elected who shall fire the world
> With consecrated hate and sacrifice,
> Leaving it warm for knowledge, and for love.[34]

Urging her to flee with him, as the house will soon be a mass
of flames, he hopes that she will "light for blinded man the fire
of truth." Her dream has been to make the blind see. Interpret-
ing her refusal to go with him as an intention to remain and
die, he rushes toward her, only to be stabbed. An immediate
realization sweeps over him—he knows she cannot die. His life
would be continued folly.

> . . . It's well for folly
> That centuries are so many, and far to count.
> Fools against fools have a long time to fight.[35]

> .   .   .

> Zoë, alone,
> Fled upward through the darkness.[36]

---

[33] *Ibid.*, pp. 103-4.   [34] *Ibid.*, p. 105.
[35] *Ibid.*, p. 109.   [36] *Ibid.*, p. 110.

She has fulfilled her duty and is again alone.

Like Hamlet, King Jasper found himself with a burden he could neither endure nor throw off. He realized that he owed something to the past and to posterity; he saw no conflict between his aims as an individual and the demands of society. But for him the will to power was paramount. As Goethe depicts Hamlet in *Wilhelm Meister*, circumstances drive him forward according to a plan of fate. It progresses from horror to horror and culminates in tragedy.

The tragedy is expressed also by Aristotle in the *Ethics*, where "a king is not a king unless he is self-sufficient and superior to his subjects in all that is good; but if he is such, there is nothing more that he needs. Hence he will consider not his own interest but the interest of his subjects; for if he were not a king after this fashion, he would be a sort of king of the ballot." [37]

If conscience is taken to be a warning of possible evil effects in the future due to wrongdoing in the present or future and if it may be at the same time actual (that is, the evil effect of wrongdoing in the past), two kinds of conscientious fears are possible; the fear of subsequent events if we follow a particular path and the fear of consequent events because we have already followed the wrong path. King Jasper suffers from the latter type. He has used Hebron as a stepping stone. It is with this in mind that Robinson portrayed Jasper as climbing from rock to rock in his dream. Jasper's dream of ambition, or climb to power, in actual life is rewarded by the detested climb to doom in his dream world. Instead of the lesser fear that he fail in his duties as a ruler, Jasper suffers greater fear because

[37] Welldon, *Ethics of Aristotle*, Book VIII, chap. xii, p. 267.

he has already failed in friendship to the elder Hebron. He has failed also as king over the younger Hebron and his generation by failing to impress them with his power and their duties toward it.

Zoë, the spirit of understanding and vitality,[38] is the most important influence in the poem and comes from another world which raises her above the limitations and dooms of the struggle for power. The dragon itself may be any or all the evils of existing society. In the poem the dragon is ill and seems to get no better as time goes on. We assume that with the destruction of the chimneys as existing forms, the dragon—the attendant evil of these forms—has been destroyed. Its illness might symbolize the ills of the social and economic structure, a structure over which Jasper was powerless.

Young Hebron, the revolutionary, in his turn hates the king for the injustice he has done his father and indirectly, but effectively, done to him. He knows only hate and his conscience precludes fear. His duty is to avenge his father, but he is no Hamlet. He hates the king as an obstacle in his own path of progress, even as the king disliked his father. Hebron's conscience is inflamed because of his love for his father and his love of justice, but this love, tantamount to passion, so blinds

---

[38] The following comment by Robinson, recorded by Hermann Hagedorn, should be noted carefully:
"Zoë isn't intended to symbolize Life . . . Zoë is knowledge, and the child of King Jasper, who is ignorance. . . . Without ignorance, there can be no knowledge." Hagedorn, *Edwin Arlington Robinson*, p. 370.
Despite this authoritative interpretation, it is important to remember Robinson's customary irony and to reflect that in the poem the "free" intelligence of Zoë is coupled with the younger generation's inability to understand the fears of their elders, with a total disregard of conscience, and responsibility, and in general with the kind of "emancipation" which springs from vitality than from reason, more from intelligent unconcern than from reflective experience.

him that he sees nothing and rights no wrongs. His love for justice, coupled with his blind hate for the doers of injustice, results merely in further evil.

Similarly, Jasper's love for his family so blinds his conscience and vision that he yields to ambition, which subsequently ruins him. The king had not been wise enough to foresee that power stolen from another would not yield pleasure to his son. The prince's love is more wholesomely directed. Although it lacks the ideal aspect of duty and is merely admiration for beauty, he at least is considerate of his parents. Likewise, while he disapproves of what his father has done, he is always solicitous for his well-being.

In analyzing the characters in *King Jasper* we see the conflict of morality as pure duty on the one hand and intelligence on the other. From the psychological, rather than the moral, point of view, the queen is the best example of "bad" conscience. She has a devoted craving to be in Jasper's presence and to provide for his welfare. She fears the hands because they can injure the object of her love. The hands, aside from their moral implications, were the threatening evil. She is weary and dreads the effect of their activity. But she does not fear Hebron. The hands and the power behind them are much larger and more deserving of fear in its broader sense. For Hebron she knows only hate—an intense aversion accompanied by a desire to destroy him. Just as she fears the destructive potentialities of the hands, so she fears the constructive tendencies of Zoë. But she does not understand growth, with its combination of creation of the old and destruction of the old, as improvement. For her it is the end of her world, and it is natural that with this point of view she should fear Zoë as the power behind the throne. Her love for her son is neither strong nor obvious, unless we interpret her attitude toward Zoë as one of jealousy for a displaced love. She had feared for the king because she felt that retribution awaited him for what she knew he had done. Her love is more apparent as her fear increases. While to the reader her suicide may appear to be the result of insurmountable difficulties, she may have rationalized that she was being considerate to both Jaspers, who no longer had room for her. Her manner of death may have been an expression of conscience rather than of selfishness or frustration.

Each character in his own way had striven for freedom. Each had realized it differently. The queen felt she was not free because of her insurmountable conscious fear of the hands. Her freedom—the freedom of a troubled conscience—came through death. The king's freedom came as soon as he realized that there was nothing to fear—that the retribution he had always feared had overtaken him. With it came light, understanding, and relief. It may seem paradoxical, but his freedom came as his power was overwhelmed by Hebron's.

Young Jasper knew very little freedom. Although he preferred to be with Zoë, his duty kept him with his parents. Even if he had escaped and gone with her, he would probably have felt that he owed his parents his attention. Hebron, while he seemed master of the most freedom, actually had the least freedom. He was constantly goaded by a desire—whether of revenge, love, or reform. He may have been free from a consciousness of fear, but this freedom was compensated for by an acute consciousness of hate that drove him on to a tragic result. Only Zoë enjoyed real freedom, and that was because she had no earthly ties. The temporary tie with the prince disturbed her customary happiness. She personified the freedom that comes with the developed powers of the intellect and the greater power of aloneness. Unlike the others, Zoë never had to subject her will to the will of others. Strange spirit that she was, she had no need to fear, or hate, or love. Unlike the others, no suffering, no sacrifice was ever demanded of her; perhaps because the only pain she had ever caused others was beneficial. Zoë's self-devotion was necessary for her continued devotion to mankind collectively, through individual man—and, strangely, this happiness could only be developed if she continued to be alone.

Bibliography

THIS CALENDAR of published works is included for the reader's convenience despite the fact that more complete lists can be found in *A Bibliography of Edwin Arlington Robinson*, by Charles Beecher Hogan, and in *A Bibliography of the Writings and Criticisms of Edwin Arlington Robinson*, by Lillian Lippincott.

Poetry and Plays by Edwin Arlington Robinson

1896

The Torrent and the Night Before. Cambridge, Mass. Printed for the author. 44 pp.

1897

The Children of the Night; a Book of Poems. Boston. 121 pp.

1899

"Menoetes," in Harvard Lyrics, selected by Charles Livingstone Stebbins. Boston. p. 111.

1902

Captain Craig; a Book of Poems. Boston and New York. 171 pp.

1910

The Town Down the River; a Book of Poems. New York. 129 pp.

1914

Van Zorn; a Comedy in Three Acts. New York. 164 pp.

1915

The Porcupine; a Drama in Three Acts. New York. 152 pp.

BIBLIOGRAPHY

1916

The Man against the Sky; a Book of Poems. New York. 149 pp.

1917

Merlin; a Poem. New York. 168 pp.

1920

Lancelot; a Poem. New York. 184 pp.
The Three Taverns; a Book of Poems. New York. 120 pp.

1921

Avon's Harvest. New York. 65 pp.
"The Pilgrims' Chorus," in The Pilgrim Spirit. Boston. pp. 77–78.
Not printed elsewhere.
Collected Poems. New York. 591 pp.

1922

"Quatrain," in A Wreath for Edwin Markham; Tributes from the
Poets of America on His Seventieth Birthday. Chicago. p. 20.

1923

Roman Bartholow. New York. 191 pp.

1924

The Man Who Died Twice. New York. 79 pp.

1925

Dionysus in Doubt; a Book of Poems. New York. 117 pp.

1927

Tristram. New York. 210 pp.

1928

Three Poems. Cambridge. 24 pp. Privately printed.
Fortunatus. Reno. 3 pp.
Sonnets 1889–1927. New York. 89 pp.

1929

Modred; a Fragment. New York. 18 pp.
Cavender's House. New York. 103 pp.
The Prodigal Son. Random House, New York. 5 pp.
Collected Poems. New York. 1018 pp.

1930

The Glory of the Nightingales. New York. 82 pp.
"The First Seven Years," in The Colophon—Part Four (December), pp. 71–78. Not printed elsewhere.
The Valley of the Shadow. San Francisco. 7 pp.

1931

Selected Poems, with a Preface by Bliss Perry. New York. 304 pp.
Matthias at the Door. New York. 99 pp.

1932

Nicodemus; a Book of Poems. New York. 90 pp.

1933

Talifer. New York. 98 pp.

1934

Amaranth. New York. 105 pp.

1935

King Jasper. New York. 110 pp.
Slumber Song (Music). Words by Louis Ledoux. Boston. 3 pp.

1936

"Too Much Coffee," in Modern American Poetry; a Critical Anthology, by Louis Untermeyer. New York. p. 146. Not printed elsewhere.
Hannibal Brown. Buffalo. 1936. 1 p. Posthumously printed.

BIBLIOGRAPHY

Prose, Including Published Letters

1897

[Excerpt from Letter to the Editor], *The Bookman,* V (March), 7. Reprinted in B. R. Redman, *Edwin Arlington Robinson,* p. 33.

1915

"Autobiographical Sketch," in Harvard, Class of 1895, Fifth Report. Cambridge. pp. 272–73. Not printed elsewhere.

1916

"The Peterborough Idea," *The North American Review,* CCIV (September), 448–54.

1917

"Remarks on Poetry," in Literature in the Making by Some of Its Makers, with Introduction by Joyce Kilmer. New York. pp. 266–73.
"Remarks on Poetry," in The Young Idea, by Lloyd R. Morris. New York. pp. 193–96. Not printed elsewhere.

1918

"A New England Poet," *The Boston Evening Transcript,* Part III (March 30), 7. Reprinted in Hogan, A Bibliography of Edwin Arlington Robinson, pp. 176–78.

1920

"Autobiographical Sketch," in Harvard, Class of 1895, Sixth Report. Cambridge. p. 411.
"From Mr. Robinson," Book review section of *The New York Times* (January 4), p. 4. Reprinted in Hogan, A Bibliography of Edwin Arlington Robinson, p. 178.

1921

[Letter], in Year Book of the Poetry Society of South Carolina. Charleston. p. 18.

1924

[Letter to Alice Hunt Bartlett], *The Poetry Review* (London), XV (January-February), 36. Reprinted in Hogan, A Bibliography of Edwin Arlington Robinson, p. 179.

"Pleasing Letter from Edwin Arlington Robinson regarding the New England Sonnet," *The Gardiner Journal* (February 14), p. 1. Reprinted in Hogan, A Bibliography of Edwin Arlington Robinson, pp. 179–80.

"Remarks on Poetry," in People You Know, by Young Boswell. New York. pp. 221–23.

1925

"A Note on Myron B. Benton," in Thoreau's Last Letter with a Note on his Correspondent, Myron B. Benton, Troutbeck Leaflets, No. 5. New York. pp. 9–12. Not printed elsewhere.

"Macdowell's Legacy to Art," Book review section of *The New York Times* (February 22), p. 2. Reprinted in Hogan, A Bibliography of Edwin Arlington Robinson, pp. 180–84.

[Tribute to Percy MacKaye], Editorial section of *The World*, New York (March 15), p. 3. Reprinted in Percy MacKaye; a Symposium, p. 44.

"Autobiographical Sketch," in Harvard, Class of 1895, Seventh Report. Cambridge. pp. 248–49. Not printed elsewhere.

1927

"A Tribute to Franklin L. Schenck," *Northport Observer*, Northport, N.Y. (February 18), p. 9.

1928

"Foreword," in Paintings by Franklin L. Schenck (1856–1927). New York. p. 4. Not printed elsewhere.

1929

Letters of Thomas Sergeant Perry, Edited with an Introduction by Edwin Arlington Robinson. New York. 14 pp.

BIBLIOGRAPHY

1931

[Excerpt from Letter to the Macmillan Company], Book section of the *Boston Evening Transcript* (October 3), p. 8. Reprinted in Hogan, A Bibliography of Edwin Arlington Robinson, p. 184.

"Introductory Letter," in Wind in the Grass, by Christy MacKaye. New York. p. 5.

1932

[Letters and remarks on "This Fine-Pretty World"], in Annals of an Era, by Percy MacKaye. Washington, D.C., p. 58.

[Letter], in On the Meaning of Life, by Will Durant. pp. 47–49. Not printed elsewhere.

"Vachel Lindsay," *The Elementary English Review*, IX (May), 115. Reprinted in Hogan, A Bibliography of Edwin Arlington Robinson, pp. 184–85.

[Letter to Edna Davis Romig], *The University of Colorado Studies*, XIX (June), 318. Reprinted in Hogan, A Bibliography of Edwin Arlington Robinson, pp. 185–86.

[Excerpt from Letter to Albert O. Bassuk], *Youth*, Brooklyn (June), p. 4. Reprinted in Hogan, A Bibliography of Edwin Arlington Robinson, p. 186.

1933

[Excerpt from Letter to William Rose Benét], in Fifty Poets. New York. p. 16.

[Letter to S. S. Alberts], A Bibliography of the Works of Robinson Jeffers. New York. p. 24. Not printed elsewhere.

[Letter to Patience B. Clarke], Magazine section of *The Lewiston Journal* (Lewiston, Me.), (October 28), p. 1. Reprinted in Hogan, A Bibliography of Edwin Arlington Robinson, p. 186.

1934

"Foreword," in The Mountain, by Carty Ranck. Rock Island, Ill. pp. 3–5. Not printed elsewhere.

"Thomas Sergeant Perry," in the Dictionary of American Biography. New York. pp. 493–94. Not printed elsewhere.

1935

[Excerpts from three letters to Laura E. Richards], *New York Herald Tribune Books* (May 12), pp. 10, 17. Reprinted in Richards, E.A.R., pp. 53-55.

1936

[Five Letters to Daniel Gregory Mason], *The Yale Review*, XXV (June), 860-64.

Edwin Arlington Robinson, A Collection of His Works From the Library of Bacon Collamore. Hartford. 68 pp. Privately printed.

[Excerpt from letter to the editors], in Chief Modern Poets of England and America. New York. p. 387. Not printed elsewhere.

[Excerpts from Six Letters to Carl Van Doren], *Harper's Magazine*, CLXXIII (July), 154-55. Reprinted in Van Doren's Three Worlds, pp. 160-62, 205-6.

[Letter to Chard Powers Smith, dated July 8, 1934], in Prelude to Man, by Chard Powers Smith. Mount Vernon, p. 13.

[Excerpt from letter to Boris Todrin], in The Room by the River, by Boris Todrin. Chicago. Printed on inside front flap of the dust wrapper.

Bibliographies

Beebe, L. M., and Robert J. Bulkley, Jr., A Bibliography of Edwin Arlington Robinson. Cambridge. 1931. 59 pp.

Hogan, Charles Beecher, A Bibliography of Edwin Arlington Robinson. New Haven. 1936. 221 pp.

Lippincott, Lillian, A Bibliography of the Writings and Criticisms of Edwin Arlington Robinson. Boston. 1937. 86 pp.

Literary Criticisms

"A Modern Allegory" [editorial], *The Times Literary Supplement*, London, No. 1722 (January 31, 1935), 58.

Arns, Karl, *Germanisch-Romanische Monatsschrift*, Heidelberg, XII (July-August, 1924), 224-33.

Benét, William Rose, "The Phoenix Nest," *The Saturday Review of Literature*, XI (April 13, 1935), 628.

Brown, Rollo Walter, Next Door to a Poet. New York. 1937. 97 pp.

Cestre, Charles, An Introduction to Edwin Arlington Robinson. New York. 1930. 230 pp.

—— "L'Œuvre poétique d'Edwin Arlington Robinson," *Revue Anglo Américaine* (Paris), I (April, 1924), 279–94.

Colum, Mary M., "Poets and Their Problems," *Forum*, XCIII (June, 1935), 343–44.

[Cowley, Malcolm], "The Week," *The New Republic*, LXXXII (April 17, 1935), 268–69.

Evans, Nancy, "Record of an Interview," *The Bookman*, LXXV (November, 1932), 675–81.

Hagedorn, Hermann, Edwin Arlington Robinson. New York. 1938. 402 pp.

Hillyer, Robert, "Amaranth," *The New England Quarterly*, VIII (March, 1935), 113–14.

Hutchinson, Percy, "The Poetry of E. A. Robinson," Book review section of *The New York Times*, April 21, 1935, pp. 2, 11.

Lowell, Amy, "Edwin Arlington Robinson," in Tendencies in Modern American Poetry. New York. 1917. pp. 67–68.

Mather, F. J., "E. A. Robinson: Poet," *The Saturday Review of Literature*, VI (January 11, 1930), 629–30.

Morris, Lloyd, The Poetry of Edwin Arlington Robinson. New York. 1923. 116 pp.

Perry, Bliss, "Poets Celebrate E. A. Robinson's Birthday—A Sheaf of Appreciative Tributes on his Fiftieth Anniversary," Book review section of *The New York Times* (December 21, 1919), p. 1.

Redman, Ben Ray, Edwin Arlington Robinson. New York, 1928. 96 pp.

Richards, Laura, E.A.R. Cambridge. 61 pp.

Roosevelt, Theodore, "The Children of the Night," *The Outlook*, LXXX (August 12, 1905), 913–14.

Untermeyer, Louis, American Poetry Since 1900. New York. 1923. pp. 42–66.

Van Doren, Carl, Three Worlds. New York. 1936. pp. 160–62.

Van Doren, Mark, Edwin Arlington Robinson. Binghamton, N.Y. 1927. 90 pp.

[Van Doren, Mark], "Edwin Arlington Robinson," *The Nation,*
CXL (April 17, 1935), 434.
Walton, Eda Lou, "Defeated Aspirations," *New York Herald Tribune Books* (October 7, 1934), p. 21.

Index

Absolute, conception of the, 25, 26, 28 f.

Adams, Franklin P., 19

Agatha, *see The Glory of the Nightingales*

Amaranth (Robinson), 127; analysis of, 22, 35, 36, 37, 44, 71-85; not an attempt to refute pessimism, 71; search for peace or resignation after maladjustment, 71; compared with *The Man against the Sky* and *The Valley of the Shadow*, 71, 72; reception, 82, 85*n;* tragedy and comedy linked inseparably, 83; indicates philosophical development, 85

Ambition, treatment of theme, 68, 70, 129 ff.

American civilization, criticism of, 123-28

Ampersand, *see Amaranth*

Aristotle, on ideal king, 140

Arns, Karl, criticism of Robinson's poetry, 23

Art, function in life, 16, 44, 83; attitude toward free, 77

Arthurian legends, treatment of, 37 f., 86-95

Atlas, *see Amaranth*

Atropos, role of Fate, 47

Benét, William Rose, attitude toward Robinson, 21

Benton, Myron B., Robinson's attitude toward, 16, 18

Biographical clues, 3-19

Blackmore, Richard Doddridge, 7

Bookman, The, article, 20

Brontë, Emily, *Wuthering Heights,* 13

Burnham, George, friendship with Robinson, 13

Burroughs, John, 18

Calvinism, intuition of original sin, 26; doctrine of election, 102

Capitalism, disintegration of, 129

Captain Craig (Robinson), 86; analysis of, 22, 35, 37, 43-55; on man's importance, 43; concept of a laughing God, 43 ff.; dream-vision of the Fates, 47; self-analysis in, 48; emphasis on loyalty to truth, 52; man's dependence on man, 53-55

Castles and love, *see* Love and castles

Cause and effect in natural justice, 102

Cavender's House (Robinson), analysis of, 30, 38, 96-102; in direct contrast with *The Glory of the Nightingales*, 96; quest for meaning of life, 99, 100; nature's scheme of justice, 102

Cestre, Charles, analysis of Robinson's poetry, 22, 23*n*

Change, role of, in *Merlin*, 90

Children of the Night, The (Robinson), 36

Christianity, Grail motif, 40, 86, 88, 91, 93, 94, 95; philosophy of will, 95; themes of salvation, forgiveness, and repentance, 102

Circumstances determine action, 136

Civil law, as adjunct of natural law, 102

Clotho, function of Fate, 47

INDEX

INDEX

Captain Craig, 22, 35, 37, 43-55, 86
Cavender's House, 30, 38, 96-102
The Children of the Night, 36
Demos and Dionysus, 39, 40
Dionysus in Doubt, 7, 39, 40, 123-28
early triolet, 6
The Glory of the Nightingales, 38, 45, 96, 99, 103-10
King Jasper, 39, 71, 95, 124, 126, 128-44
Lancelot, 19, 37, 86
The Man against the Sky, 15, 27, 35, 36, 49, 55-63, 71, 81
The Man Who Died Twice, 35, 44, 49, 63-71
Matthias at the Door, 19, 27, 38, 39, 110-17
Merlin, 19, 22, 25, 37 f., 86-95
The Night Before, 11
"Peterborough Idea," 16
The Porcupine, 38, 39
Talifer, 38, 39, 117-22
The Three Taverns, 36
The Torrent and the Night Before, 20, 36
The Town Down the River, 22, 36
Tristram, 3, 37
Two Sonnets, 32
The Valley of the Shadow, 36, 44, 58, 71, 72
Van Zorn, 38, 39
Romanticism, Robinson's realistic reinterpretation of, 37
Roosevelt, Franklin Delano, 128
Roosevelt, Theodore, 13, 14
Royce, Josiah, influence, 8, 11, 25-34, 52, 53, 95; *The Spirit of Modern Philosophy*, 8, 27 f.; rationalized interpretation of life, 26; interpretation of Schopenhauer, 28-30; attitude toward loyalty, 95
Rule, *see* Government

Sanger, John, 5
Santayana, George, influence, 24, 32; *The Last Puritan*, 32
Schopenhauer, Arthur, influence, 24,

25, 28-34, 52, 83, 94; Roycean interpretation of, 28
Science, interest in, 56, 86; difference between poetry and, 84; attitude of man of, toward life, 118
Self, problem of knowing, 31, 32-34, 39, 40, 46, 71 ff.; 83, 85; treatment of self-accusation, 96-102; self-pity or laughter? 115; efficacy of assertion of, 121; misdirected freedom a limit on expression of, 124
Sexual love, *see* Love
Shadows, *see* Light and shadows
Shakespeare, William, 6
Sin, treatment of, in *Merlin*, 87
Skepticism, traces of, 11, 35, 36, 63, 82, 88*n*, 114
Social theme, 39 f., 123 ff.; society and individual, 140
Socrates, on genius of comedy and tragedy in *Symposium*, 83
"Specks" motif in *Merlin*, 87, 90
Spencer, Herbert, influence, 31, 102
Spinoza, Baruch, attitude toward, 5
Spirit of Modern Philosophy, The (Royce), influence, 8, 27 f.
State, *see* Government
Sterling, George, attitude toward Robinson's poetry, 21
Styx, Doctor, *see* *Amaranth*
Success and failure, attitude toward, 5, 9 f., 14, 15, 18, 53, 70, 111
Suicide, attitude toward, 35, 66, 71, 79, 81, 83; alternative to, and absolute faith, 56, 60, 71
Sun, devil in the, 50
Symposium (Plato), Socrates on genius of comedy and tragedy, 83

Talifer (Robinson), analysis of, 38, 39, 117-22; comedy of love, 117; attainment of happiness, 118, 121; evaluation of knowledge and ignorance, 120
Tavern of the Vanquished in *Amaranth*, 73 ff.
Tennyson, Alfred, 6

[161]